The History

of

UNION
WHARF

1793–1998

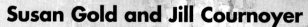

Susan Gold and Jill Cournoyer

Custom Communications/Publisher
Saco, Maine

Portland, Me. — Evening on Portland Harbor.

Published by Custom Communications, 92 Franklin St., Saco, ME 04072
(207) 286–9295. E-mail: history@desktoppub.com. Web site:http://www.desktoppub.com

Library of Congress Cataloging-in-Publication Data
Gold, Susan Dudley.
The history of Union Wharf, 1793–1998 / Susan Gold and Jill Cournoyer.
      p.   cm.
Includes index.
ISBN 1-892168-01-4.
1. Union Wharf (Portland, Me.) —History. 2. Portland (Me.)—History.
I. Cournoyer, Jill, 1957- . II. Title.
HE554.P84G65   1998
387.1'09741'91—dc21   98-28345
                                                    CIP

Summary: An in-depth history of Union Wharf, its founders, and its times from 1793 to present day. Also highlights the contributions of the Shurtleff and Poole families, prominent in the development and growth of the wharf and its parent corporation, the Proprietors of Union Wharf. Focuses on Portland, Maine.

Illustration and Photo Credits
Provided by the Poole family: Cover illustration and pages 1; 8; 44 *t*, *b*; 45 *t*; 46 *b*; 48 *t*, *b*; 49 *b*; 90 *b*; 92 *b*. Philip Gemmer: 4. Don Johnson: Back cover photograph, 108. MN Co. postcard: 2. The Hugh C. Leighton Co.: 9, 46 *t*. Lisa Mead: 6 and 7 *b*. Office of the Chief of Engineers, United States Army (1820): 6 and 7 *t*. Brian Peterson (courtesy of City of Portland's Department of Transportation and Waterfront: 92 *t*; 93 *t*, *b*. The Portland Newspapers: 10; 91 *t*, *b* (Doug Jones); 18, 82 (Charles Merrill); 90 *t* (Peter Darling). W.H. Shurtleff Co.: 40; 47 *t*, *b*. Collections of the Maine Historical Society: 44 *m*; 49 *t*. Cole Land Transportation Museum: 45 *b*.

Design, Typography, and Setup
Custom Communications
First Edition
Printed in the United States of America.
10 9 8 7 6 5 4 3 2 1

Acknowledgments

Many people have contributed to this history. We would like to thank them for their patience and efforts in seeing this project to completion. Our heartfelt thanks go to the following:

- Charles Poole, William Poole, and Malcolm Poole, for sharing anecdotes and keen observations of their family, Union Wharf, and the W.H. Shurtleff Company.
- Victoria Poole, who provided much-appreciated suggestions on the manuscript.
- John Ferland, whose thesis on the Portland waterfront provided invaluable insights into the zoning and rebuilding of the port.
- Joel W. Eastman, University of Southern Maine professor, author of "The Historic Development of the Port of Portland, 1633–1990," for the *Portland Newspapers*.
- The staff of the Portland Museum of Art for their research assistance.
- William D. Barry of the Maine Historical Society for his assistance and knowledgeable advice.
- Linda Madsen, librarian for the *Portland Newspapers*, for her help in photo research.
- The research staff at Portland Public Library's Portland Room for their assistance and advice.
- Nathan Lipford of the Maine Maritime Museum for sharing his expertise on ships and ship registration.

Parker Poole Jr. in 1988

- The research staff at Greater Portland Landmarks for their assistance.

Most of all, we would like to thank Parker Poole Jr., whose support for the project and unflagging enthusiasm kept us all on track. Without his appreciation of the value of recording Union Wharf's history for future generations, this book would not have been possible.

Thank you all.

Susan Gold
Jill Cournoyer

Dedication

Dedicated to the fifteen Poole grandchildren:

Malcolm Augustus Poole
Elizabeth Folinsbee Poole
Stuart Wiggins Poole
Parker Poole IV
Christopher Talcott Poole
William Andrew Poole
Hollister A. Poole
Emily O'Brien Poole
Harold Riker Poole
Jonathan Simes Poole
Victoria McCormick Thomas
Rebecca Poole Thomas
Anne Briscoe Thomas
Charlotte Westwood Sawyer
Hannah Rines Sawyer

You are the stewards of the past and the standard bearers of the future.

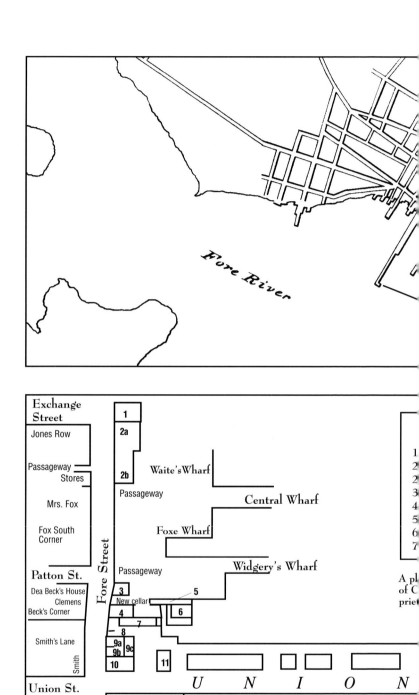

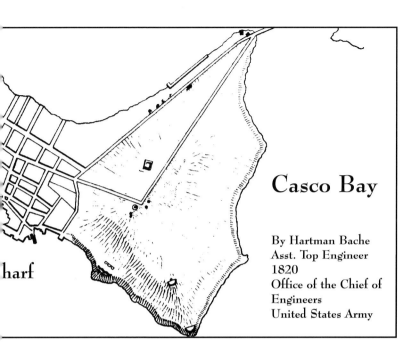

Casco Bay

By Hartman Bache
Asst. Top Engineer
1820
Office of the Chief of
Engineers
United States Army

harf

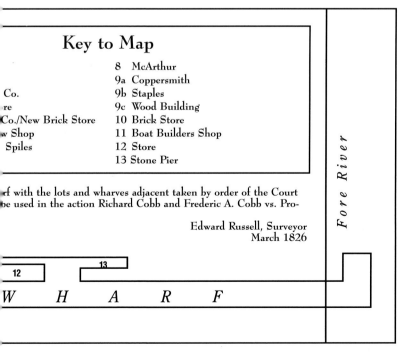

Key to Map

Co.
re
Co./New Brick Store
w Shop
Spiles

8   McArthur
9a Coppersmith
9b Staples
9c Wood Building
10 Brick Store
11 Boat Builders Shop
12 Store
13 Stone Pier

rf with the lots and wharves adjacent taken by order of the Court
be used in the action Richard Cobb and Frederic A. Cobb vs. Pro-

Edward Russell, Surveyor
March 1826

Fore River

12

13

W   H   A   R   F

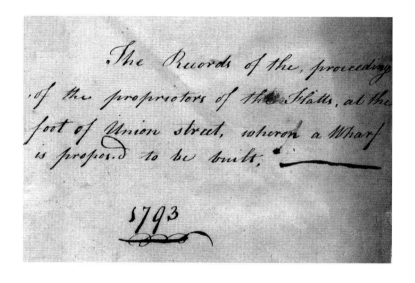

The Records of the proceedings of the proprietors of the Flatts, at the
foot of Union street, wheron a Wharf is proposed to be built.   1793

—from the first page of the 1793 Union Wharf record book

CONTENTS

INTRODUCTION
From Pirates to Parking Lots   *11*

CHAPTER I
Building a Wharf   *19*

CHAPTER II
Old West Indies Trade   *41*

CHAPTER III
Rise of the Railroad   *59*

CHAPTER IV
Port in Decline   *83*

CHAPTER V
Renovation and Renewal   *109*

INDEX   *127*

Introduction

From Pirates to Parking Lots

I n early 1994, dozens of partygoers gathered at 36 Union Wharf in Portland, Maine, to toast the two hundredth anniversary of the wharf, built over the Fore River in 1793. For wharfinger Parker Poole Jr. it was a triumphant moment, the culmination of a two-decade-long effort to rejuvenate the oldest existing wharf in Portland.

When Poole took the reins of the wharf from his father, Parker Poole Sr., in 1964, the dock—cluttered and rundown—showed its age. Poole demolished nearly all the aging, dilapidated buildings on the pier and replaced them with modern, fireproof ones. He attracted a mixture of tenants to complement the fishing and marine-related businesses. Poole took particular pride in the fact that his ancestors had been associated with the wharf for more than 120 years. The wharf's renewal assured the continuing existence of an enterprise that had survived more than two centuries of changing markets, weather, and leadership.

Union Wharf began at a time of great hope and promise

for a young country. The maritime trade along the East Coast linked the newly independent colonies to the world and to each other. Seaport towns flourished, as shipping-related businesses, from boatbuilding to ship brokerage offices to sailors' boarding houses, grew. In 1793, ships loading and unloading cargo dotted the Portland waterfront. The Neck, as that area was then called, bustled with activity. The port, a deep, natural harbor with easy access to land and shelter from storms, was fast developing into a major trading center. Though the population in the surrounding area was smaller than in the port cities of Boston and New York, Portland had the advantage of being closer to England than its larger rivals.

Buoyant with the post-Revolutionary spirit of enterprise, groups of local men of the sea trade joined together to build wharves to serve the increasing number of vessels visiting Portland Harbor. Union Wharf, erected in 1793 by a group calling itself the Proprietors of Union Wharf, became the first full-length pier to extend into Fore River. An extension of Union Street located about halfway between the eastern and western ends of the Portland waterfront, Union Wharf soon became home to a dozen wooden stores and sheds built to hold goods coming from and going to England, the West Indies, and China.

For the next two hundred years and beyond, Union Wharf weathered the tides of the shipping and sea trade industries in Maine and the world. Today Union remains on duty as Portland's oldest wharf. With its modern buildings and facilities, the wharf continues as a hub of marine trade as it prepares to enter the twenty-first century.

The Portland of the 1790s, when Union Wharf was built,

was a city of great promise. The young nation's economy depended on the marine trade to bring in supplies and to sell American goods overseas. The seaports of the Northeast—including Portland (then called Falmouth)—played a major role in the robust economic activity taking place. Union Wharf's construction spurred entrepreneurs to build a dozen other wharves along the city's waterfront.

Through most of the 1800s, the wharves were alive with the sights of sails and masts towering above the water and the sounds of stevedores yelling and singing as they loaded and unloaded rum, molasses, sugar, and grain. Well-built and maintained by the Proprietors, Union Wharf remained at the center of this hubbub.

The wharf was also involved in the controversies and the crises of the times. In 1807, dissenters against the federal Embargo Act that prohibited trade with other countries launched a protest ship from Union Wharf. It earned a footnote in history books during the War of 1812 when the bodies of two captains killed during a sea battle off the Maine coast were brought to the wharf. Mourners gathered on Union Wharf for an impromptu funeral for the two heroes, one from each side of the battle. During that war, Union Wharf businessmen launched the *Dash*, one of the most famous privateer ships of the era.

In 1850, the city laid a new road, aptly named Commercial Street, through the middle of the wharves. Railroad tracks on the street linked the wharves to Canadian trade through the Grand Trunk Railroad and to U.S. trade through the Maine Central Railroad. The chugging and clanking of locomotives soon competed with the creaking of ships' masts in the harbor.

Making the most of the modern technology, the Proprietors laid rails on Union Wharf to link the mainland's trains and the port's seagoing vessels. The railroad cars unloaded their goods for export overseas and loaded up with cargo that had sailed the ocean from foreign lands.

Over the years, the vessels docking alongside the wharf changed, as different ships fit different times. In the early 1800s, the huge, graceful square riggers with their towering sails dominated the skyline. They traveled the trade route to and from the West Indies, carrying molasses, sugar, and lumber, weathering storms at sea, and fighting off pirates and British and French warships. When news of the California gold rush hit New England in the late 1840s, speedy clipper ships launched from the wharf. They looped around the often treacherous Cape Horn en route to the Western frontier. In the 1820s, passenger steamboats left the pier for pleasure trips to nearby islands. Later in the century, steamships carried salt from the Mediterranean and the West Indies and coal from Pennsylvania. Fishing vessels and lobster boats, bobbing alongside the wharf, became a constant fixture. In the 1990s, a state-of-the-art, 208-foot, diesel-powered vessel designed to respond to oil spills took up residence at the west end of the pier.

Through all these myriad changes, the Proprietors of Union Wharf posted dividends for their shareholders almost every year, proving to be not only able sea captains but shrewd businessmen as well. They instituted rules and set wharfage rates to regulate the flow of business along the pier. In 1856 they incorporated themselves to establish a stronger legal identity. Most of the proprietors, wharfingers (wharf managers), and members of the wharf committee came from seafaring families, among the most respected in Portland's marine community. The same names appear in the record books again and again, most notably the McLellans and the Shurtleffs—proof that the wharf has essentially been a family business, passed down from one generation to another for more than two hundred years.

By the twentieth century, the railroad and trucking industries had taken over much of the trade that had once come by sea. The decline of maritime trade hit hard along Portland's waterfront, where the privately owned wharves found little public help. After the destruction of the Great Fire of 1866, the city of Portland struggled to regain its economic footing. In rebuilding the city, public officials often neglected the waterfront in favor of promoting manufacturing and tourism. Many wharves fell into disrepair. Once a bustling trade center and gathering spot of the city's elite, the waterfront became an eyesore of crumbling buildings and rotting planks amid a tangle of weeds.

The Proprietors of Union Wharf responded by attracting a diversity of tenants and by reinvesting millions of dollars in an aggressive rebuilding program on the four-acre wharf. In the first decades of the twentieth century, they built one of the best coal handling operations in New England and distributed the fuel throughout the region until the late 1940s. In the 1980s, the wharf corporation merged with former Union Wharf tenant W.H. Shurtleff Company, the salt and chemical firm that had long played a major role in the wharf's development. The consolidation strengthened both enterprises.

Brown Ship Chandlery, owned by the Proprietors of Union Wharf, became a major addition to the wharf complex in the

1980s. The wharf owners invested in real estate, buying property on neighboring Widgery's Wharf and Richardson Wharf as well as expanding their land holdings. They tore down dilapidated buildings to make way for a profitable parking lot and built modern structures to suit prospective tenants.

A 1983 city ordinance that set aside the waterfront area for marine businesses only posed a threat to wharf owners, including the Proprietors of Union Wharf. Viewing the new law as merely a bump along the road, the Proprietors took a chapter from their ancestors' book on adapting to changing markets and times. They opened the Union Wharf Chandlery & Market at the head of the wharf to serve local fishermen and other mariners and sought out new marine-only tenants.

From pirates to parking lots, Union Wharf's story is a tale of the sea, of sailors, of trade and commerce. Its history is intimately entwined with the events of the last two hundred years. Centuries-old record books reveal narratives of fortitude and foresight among the astute business leaders who built and maintained the wharf during a time when people had to take great risks to succeed in a world governed by nature. Union Wharf was created when the nation was but a decade old; it has weathered a civil war, two world wars, and numerous conflicts. Tall clipper ships, steamers, and diesel-powered vessels have visited its docks; horse-drawn carts, horseless carriages, rail cars, and front-end loaders have carried goods to and from its warehouses.

Union Wharf shares its history with that of an enterprising family, whose connection with the wharf begins more than a century ago and trails through generations to today's leaders. A.K. Shurtleff first served on a committee of the Proprietors of

Union Wharf in 1858. Members of the Shurtleff family, involved in Maine's shoe manufacturing and maritime shipping industries, have had connections to Union Wharf ever since. A.K.'s brother, Sylvan Shurtleff, operated his shoe manufacturing firm from Union Wharf. Sylvan's son, William H. Shurtleff, expanded his father's business and opened a salt storehouse on the wharf in 1890. Throughout the next century, the W.H. Shurtleff Company expanded to become one of the largest salt and chemical dealers in New England. The company left Union Wharf in 1964, but the link between the two enterprises continued under the guidance of Parker Poole Sr., Shurtleff's son-in-law. For many years, Poole served as president of both the Shurtleff Company and the Proprietors of Union Wharf. In the mid-1960s, Parker Poole Jr. assumed control of the wharf and its parent corporation, the Proprietors of Union Wharf, while his brother, William, became president of W.H. Shurtleff. Shurtleff became a wholly owned subsidiary of the Proprietors of Union Wharf in 1983. Parker's sons, Charlie and Malcolm, are the fifth generation of family members working to ensure the success of the Proprietors of Union Wharf and its subsidiary companies.

Union Wharf began 205 years ago with the simple declaration "to build a Wharf on a piece of flats, at the bottom of Union Street in Portland." That structure still stands today, its history a microcosm of the economics, politics, business, and weather of the last two centuries. This book documents the passage of Union Wharf through all the milestones of the years. It also describes the challenges of today's world and how the owners are adapting the venerable wharf to ensure that it survives well into the twenty-first century.

I

Building a Wharf

A dozen years after the Mayflower landed on the Plymouth shore, English settlers ventured to northern Massachusetts (later to become Maine) to establish a small colony along the shores of the Fore River. The residents of the fledgling community lived in wooden huts near the foot of India Street in an area known as "The Neck." In 1718, the colonists incorporated their settlement as the town of Falmouth, named after a city in their native England. They chose the Neck area along the waterfront, where about twenty families had already settled, as the center of town. The town committee called the Neck "a very agreeable place . . . most commodious for a fishery."

The settlers made their living from the sea—fishing for the plentiful cod and haddock that fed in the Gulf of Maine and shipping supplies and resources between England and America. They exchanged their main staple of trade, massive pine logs used by the British Royal Navy as masts for their fleet, for grain and other imports from England.

By 1634, seventeen ships carried on the settlers' trade with England. Merchants and seamen, attracted by the harbor's deep, well-protected port, brought their ships and their business to the burgeoning town. In 1722, more than two hundred homes dotted the land along the waterfront. Vessel owners built ten small wharves into the Fore River leading to the Atlantic Ocean to serve the growing number of ships that sailed into the harbor.

The Revolutionary War with Great Britain nearly destroyed the growing town. In 1775, a squadron of British vessels sailed into the harbor. Captain Henry Mowatt anchored his twenty-gun ship opposite the wharves. Piqued at having been briefly detained by some residents of Brunswick, Maine, Mowatt opened fire on the Neck. All 414 buildings in the town center and the port's ten wharves burned. When the smoke cleared, only one hundred homes remained standing.

Some settlers fled, but many stayed, and by 1786 the town had two thousand residents. That year, local merchants, including Arthur, Hugh, and Joseph McLellan Sr., successfully petitioned Falmouth officials to cut ties with the rest of the town and renamed the Neck area Portland. The new town soon established itself as a booming trade center, thanks in large part to a sweet, gooey mixture called molasses.

Molasses from the West Indies soon became Portland's staple import as Americans sought the sweet liquid to supplement their diets and to make rum. For almost a century, the Old West Indies trade—revolving mostly around molasses and sugar—supported generations of Maine traders, merchants, and sailors. While huge, square-rigged sailing ships brought molasses and sugar to Portland Harbor, other ships left the port carrying timber, fish, cordwood, shooks (folded-up barrels), masts, and spars for trade across the sea.

Busy Harbor

Portland Harbor was a busy place in 1793. Twenty-four brigs, twenty-three schooners, twenty sloops, and thirteen ships handled tons of cargo in the port that year. At the foot of Union Street, David Smith and Daniel Ilsley had constructed a breastworks, a crude sort of dock made of stones and rubble where ships loaded and unloaded their cargo. Ilsley also built a distillery on the breastworks to make rum from molasses.

With all the traffic going in and out of the harbor, it soon became apparent that the port needed a more permanent structure from which to load and unload ships. In 1792, a group of merchants and sea captains—including Ilsley and Smith—decided to build a wharf at the site of the breastworks. The deed to the property stated that the twenty-five group members "have agreed to build a Wharf on a piece of flatts, at the bottom of Union Street in Portland . . . and to erect stores thereupon."

Billy Mac's Piano

In the late 1700s, William McLellan ran a variety store on Temple Street near the waterfront. He carried many objects, including pianos, which he shipped to Portland from Boston. Apparently there must have been a demand for the instrument among local music lovers because McLellan asked Captain John Lewis, owner of a sloop that sailed between Boston and Portland, to bring him another "forte-piano."

When Lewis returned from Boston, he informed McLellan that he hadn't been able to find a "forty-pounder." A long thirty-two was the largest available.

"I want it taken away, as it lays right across my hatch," Lewis told McLellan. Instead of a piano, Lewis had brought the shopkeeper a gun.

For several years the gun lay at Long Wharf, where it was derisively known as "Billy Mac's piano." The "piano" proved its worth, however, when it became a pivot gun on the privateer *Dash* during the War of 1812.

The group, calling itself "Proprietors of Union Wharf," voted in 1792 to sell shares at fifty pounds each (about $700 in 1990 dollars) to raise money for materials to erect a wharf. The original proprietors divided twenty-eight shares among themselves. David Smith, Robert Boyd, Joseph Jewett, and Enoch Ilsley bought two shares each. Proprietor Nathaniel Deering had no share. The remaining proprietors, including three McLellans—Hugh, Joseph Sr., and Arthur—owned one share each. The other proprietors were Ebeneezer Storer, John Bagley, Ralph Cross, John Mussey, Woodbury Storer, Daniel Tucker, Joseph Boyd, Stephen Deblois, Thomas Webster, Thomas Buck, John Nobbey, James Jewett, Ebeneezer Preble, Stephen Codman, Jesse Sumner, Daniel Ilsley, and John Quimby.

At its first meeting, the group chose Woodbury Storer to serve as agent and wharf manager, or wharfinger, of Union Wharf. Some of the original owners immediately sold their shares to William King Esq., a Bath merchant who later became governor of Maine.

Built in 1793, Union Wharf stood as a monument to eighteenth century ingenuity. Using horse-drawn wagons, builders hauled rocks, dirt, and other fill material to the tidal land to form the base of the wharf. Massive oak pilings, dragged from Maine forests to the Portland waterfront, supported the 110-foot-wide structure covered with wide wooden planks. In all, builders used 3,502 tons of lumber for the wharf, which would eventually extend 2,200 feet over the bay.

A forty-eight-foot-wide passageway ran down the center of the wharf. On either side, five businesses, each set on a thirty-foot-wide lot, offered their wares to mariners and other customers. Among them was a retail store at 16 Union Wharf, Joseph McLellan & Son, run by Union Wharf proprietor Joseph McLellan Sr. An 1805 advertisement for the store offered customers oats, rye, flour, corn, tobacco, sea coral, glass, and wine. McLellan transported goods between Portland and Boston; Charleston, South Carolina; Liverpool, England; and the West Indies. His ships, *Joseph, Eliza,* and *Caroline;* schooners

Francis and *Prince;* and the sloop, *Venus,* carried the typical goods of the time: salt, coal, corn, rye, oats, flour, tobacco, and wooden crates.

In December 1793, the Proprietors voted to collect another thirty pounds per share from the shareholders to raise additional money for Union Wharf. They agreed to pay the wharfinger 7.5 percent on all monies collected from wharf businesses. Hugh McLellan, Daniel Foley, and William Harrinton were elected to serve on a Wharf Committee to regulate rates and anchorage and confer with owners of the other wharves then under way.

Within two years of Union Wharf's construction, fifteen stores lined the dock. As the wharf's business grew, the Proprietors wrote down rules to govern its operation. In 1797 they voted that no proprietor had exclusive privilege to land or take merchandise off Union Wharf. Mariners using the wharf were expected to run a tight ship. An 1805 rule required the master or owner of any vessel docked at the wharf to rig in the jib boom and top the lower yards when ordered to do so by the wharfinger. Those who didn't had to pay double the wharfage until they complied.

The Proprietors, meeting twice a year, regularly voted money for repairs and improvements to the wharf. In 1801, they added 156 feet to the wharf, and in 1806 they spent $150 per shareholder to extend the structure another 200 feet. An allotment of $100 per shareholder was approved in 1804 to fix up the "lower joag" (a jog is the projecting part of a wharf) and repair "the Olde Wharf"—presumably the original section of the pier. In 1805 repairs were made to the east side damaged by "late storms."

The Magnificent McLellans

The McLellans could rightfully be called the founding family of Union Wharf. In 1730, weaver Bryce McLellan left his native Ireland to settle in the coastal Maine area then known as the Neck. Bryce's sons and grandsons became leading members of Maine society at the turn of the century. All three of Bryce's sons, Joseph, William, and Arthur, were sea captains and merchants when the British burned the Neck in 1775. Joseph lost a fifty-four-ton vessel and an eighteen-ton schooner in the fire. In the long run, however, the McLellans benefited from the blaze. Many leading citizens fled after the attack, leaving sea captains like the McLellans who remained to rebuild the town and win for themselves prominent positions in society. Over the next few decades, the McLellans involved themselves in nearly every aspect of the growing waterfront town.

The founder of one of Maine's greatest shipping fleets, Joseph McLellan served as an officer during the American Revolution and signed Massachusetts' ratification of the U.S. Constitution. He and his son, Hugh, and his brother, Arthur, helped in the successful drive to separate the Neck area from Falmouth in 1786 and rename it Portland.

Hugh, Arthur, and Joseph Sr. were among the original Proprietors of Union Wharf. In 1800 the McLellans organized Maine's first bank, Portland Bank, and the state's first insurance company, Maine Fire & Insurance Company. With the formation of the local firm, area merchants no longer had to rely on the distant Lloyd's of London for their insurance needs. The McLellan family supported culture as well, providing funding for Maine's first public library.

Joseph McLellan Sr. was a crusty character who once bought up an enemy's debts and had him thrown in jail. Out on bail, the debtor, newspaper editor Thomas Wait, attacked McLellan in an article published in the Portland paper. Seeking to avenge his father, Joseph Jr., a sea captain, pommeled Wait in a public brawl.

Within this ambitious and energetic family, Joseph Sr.'s eldest son, Hugh, born in 1758, stood out. While still a young man, he amassed a fortune and built a three-story brick mansion on High Street near the waterfront, now called the McLellan-Sweat House. The list of official posts Hugh McLellan held is extensive: fire warden, town assessor, referee in maritime cases, justice of the peace, and captain of the local infantry. To aid the maritime community, he formed the Portland Marine Society, which posted news about foreign events that affected shipping and circulated lists of ships and sailors lost at sea. He also served as president of Portland Bank.

In 1807, the McLellans were at the peak of their power and influence when Congress passed the Embargo Act forbidding U.S. ships to engage in foreign trade. Like other maritime families, the McLellans were hard hit by the embargo and their fortunes quickly plunged. Henry Ilsley &

Company, owned partly by Stephen and Joseph McLellan Sr., dissolved in 1808. Another family business, Joseph McLellan & Son at 16 Union Wharf, limped along until 1813 when it was forced to close.

Hugh McLellan, showing the hubris and stubbornness that helped him rise to power, refused to obey the Embargo Act and instead continued shipping to foreign shores. With each shipment, the U.S. government took him to court, winning all seven judgments against him. Even as his debts grew, Hugh continued to speculate in business, buying Union Wharf shares from son-in-law Joseph Pope. Eventually, hard times caught up with the McLellans. Both Hugh and Stephen were forced to auction off their mansions. Joseph Jr. briefly served time in debtor's prison. The Reverend Samuel Deane of the First Parish Church spoke of the town's "broken merchants," a reference to the McLellans and others caught in the embargo imbroglio.

Though Hugh avoided the ignominy of prison by relying on his son-in-law, chandler Charles Fox, for financial help, he finally went bankrupt. He spent his last years in a modest house several streets away from his former mansion, running a grocery store on Union Street. His personal life was marred by tragedy as well: of his nine children, none of his sons survived to adulthood. In 1823, Hugh died insolvent at the age of 64. His obituary merited but a few lines in the local papers. Despite this lack of recognition, the many institutions he helped found—from Union Wharf to the Marine Society to the town's first bank and insurance company—served as monuments to his memory.

In later years, the McLellan family recovered from their misfortunes and thrived. William McLellan Jr., son of William McLellan, became a wealthy sea captain and merchant and lived in a luxurious house in Portland. Jacob McLellan, William Jr.'s son, served as Portland's mayor in the 1860s.

The McLellans continued to play a major role in the management of Union Wharf through the 1830s. Arthur McLellan was treasurer for many years, finally ending his service in 1834. Stephen and William McLellan served as wharfingers, and Thomas McLellan, Arthur's son, was wharfinger and treasurer.

A SPRIGHTLY TOWN

Business boomed at Union Wharf and the surrounding towns as the young country headed into the nineteenth century. In 1797, writer Timothy Dwight noted that no American town was more commercial or sprightly than Portland. By 1806, it had become the sixth largest seaport in the country. The United States prospered partly because European countries, at war with England, banned that nation's ships from their ports. That left the European market wide open to upstart traders from America. Profits ran high. Maine shippers paid $8 to ship one thousand pieces of lumber to Havana, Cuba, where the lot sold for $60. Meanwhile, merchants in small towns like Portland ensured that prices stayed high by unloading only a limited amount of goods and shipping the rest to Boston.

On July 9, 1805, a fire temporarily disrupted Union Wharf's prosperity. Flames consumed stores owned by three of the original proprietors of the wharf—Captain David Smith, Woodbury Storer, and Robert Boyd. The fire, which was thought to have started when someone discarded a lit cigar in one of the store lofts, also destroyed shops belonging to a tailor by the name of Wright, a hatter known as Mr. Woodman, and Mr. Hady, a blacksmith. Stores on the wharf were filled with combustible material. The fire boat couldn't reach the wharf because of low tide, but the prompt response of the town's fire brigade prevented an even worse disaster. After the fire, the three proprietors ran an advertisement in the *Eastern Argus* thanking the town and its citizens for their quick action in putting out the blaze.

At that time, William McLellan was wharfinger of Union Wharf, serving from 1804 to 1810. The McLellans were among the seafaring families who amassed large fortunes at the turn of the century. Brothers Hugh and Stephen McLellan (sons of Joseph Sr.), both sea captains, built mansions near the waterfront. The McLellans also involved themselves in community affairs. Their money helped build the Portland Observatory in 1807, where a lookout scanned the horizon through a high-powered telescope, then raised a flag to announce the arrival of each ship as it sailed into port. That year, the Proprietors of Union Wharf pledged $140 for a watchman for the protection and safety of the wharf.

EMBARGO ACT

The relationship between England and the United States

continued to deteriorate after the Revolutionary War. Still clinging to its rule of the sea, the English navy raided American ships in international waters on the pretext that British deserters were aboard. Sailors who could not prove their American citizenship became indentured servants, some forced to serve on British man-o-war ships for up to ten years. Approximately seven thousand Americans served on British vessels against their will as a result of Great Britain's "impressment" policy.

England also seized hundreds of U.S. ships outright during the early 1800s. When France went to war with Great Britain, the French adopted a similar policy toward American vessels, capturing 389 U.S. ships between 1803 and 1807. Reacting to the atrocities against American mariners, U.S. President Thomas Jefferson pushed Congress into passing the Embargo Act in December 1807. The act, which banned U.S. ships from trading overseas, was designed to punish the English and the French by depriving them of American goods, but it hurt U.S. merchants much more than their European counterparts.

With marine trade halted by the embargo, the heady days of Portland's booming economy ended abruptly. The act's effect on Portland was devastating. By December, eleven commercial houses in Portland, including Joseph McLellan & Son, couldn't pay their debts. Along Portland's waterfront, grass grew on the once-thriving wharves. Abandoned vessels rotted and sank at anchor. Public soup kettles sprang up around town to feed the starving populace.

In a town of a few thousand, three hundred people in marine-related businesses and those who had worked as sailors no longer had jobs. The duty imposed on imports coming into

Portland Harbor in 1808 plummeted to one-seventh the amount collected in 1807. The tonnage handled in the port during the fourteen-month embargo dropped from 1.5 million tons to less than ten thousand tons.

Many upstanding citizens defied the unpopular law and continued to trade with Europe. Union Wharf provided a launching point for one anti-Embargo Act rally. Protesters painted the stern and quarters of a ship with the word "embargo" spelled backwards—mockingly declaring, "O-Grab-Me." They loaded the ship onto a cart pulled by horses and paraded it through town accompanied by a band playing doleful music. The marchers, including unemployed ship masters, mates, and mechanics, assembled at Monument Square, where Captain Edward Kelleran addressed them. The dilapidated ship was then given a quick paint job and spruced up to show what would happen once the embargo ended. Riggers put the ship "in the best trim, hoisted the American ensign at each masthead, and a crew of neatly dressed sailors manned her." They paraded it to Union Wharf, where it was launched to the cheers of the large crowd. Hugh McLellan, who continued to ship in violation of the Embargo Act, was likely among those who cheered. In the ensuing court actions brought by the U.S. government, the courts ruled against him seven times and fined him a total of $7,577.43 for violating the act.

The McLellans, who had invested so much in Union Wharf, particularly suffered during the embargo. Their businesses, Joseph McLellan & Son and McLellan & Brown, could not meet their debts. Joseph Jr. sold his "fast-sailing brig" *Sampson* at auction, but he failed to raise enough money to avoid a brief stay in debtor's prison. Joseph Sr. managed to retain his stores at 16, 23, and 25 Union Wharf throughout the embargo, but most of the family money was lost.

The experience of the McLellans was not unique. Businesses up and down the eastern seaboard faced bankruptcy as their exports and ships rotted at the wharves. New England, whose economy revolved around ocean trade, threatened to secede from the Union. Pressured by desperate merchants, Congress modified the Embargo Act in 1809 to allow trade with Great Britain and France. When this did not bring things back to normal, Congress repealed the trade restrictions altogether in 1810.

The Portland waterfront slowly began to recover after Congress lifted the Embargo Act. By 1810, import duties had risen to 40 percent of 1807 amounts. Before the harbor's shipping industry could duplicate the economic boom of pre-embargo days, however, hostilities between the United States and Great Britain exploded into the War of 1812. The sea turned into a battlefield, and private merchant ships became fair game.

A DASH OF ADVENTURE

During wartime, private vessel owners obtained licenses from the government to chase and capture enemy ships and cargoes. The shipowners were allowed to keep whatever they seized. During the War of 1812, 526 American privateer ships roamed the seas looking for British prey. Most kept close to shore between Maine and Newfoundland. While a few became famous, most had little luck, with three-quarters getting no prizes or being captured themselves.

Union Wharf merchants Samuel and Seward Porter were

among those shipowners who outfitted their vessels with guns and sought to capture the enemy's cargo for the war effort and their own profit. The Porters owned one of the most famous of the privateer ships, the *Dash*, built in Freeport, Maine. The *Dash*, a 220-ton brig, was originally rigged as a topsail schooner with all the light sails it could set. A crew of forty manned the vessel's thirty-two-pound pivot gun and six guns positioned broadside. While fleeing from a British vessel during one encounter, the *Dash* broke its foremast sail. Its owners then converted the ship to a hermaphrodite brig, a two-masted sailing ship with its main mast rigged both fore and aft. During its illustrious career, the *Dash* participated in seven raids and captured fifteen British ships. A crowd cheered whenever the bellicose brig sailed from port.

In between sieges, the *Dash* transported coffee and other goods from southern ports, including Haiti, to the Porters' stockhouses in Portland. During one trip, the crew had to dump 522 of 550 bags of coffee overboard to escape a vengeful British vessel.

Before the war ended, disaster struck the Porters—not at sea but on Union Wharf. A January 2, 1814, fire decimated their four Union Wharf businesses. The merchants had not insured the tons of coffee, valued at $1 per pound, and other goods stored at their warehouse to keep them safe from the British. To raise money to rebuild their businesses, the Porters put the *Dash* up for sale at auction. On the day of the auction, however, the Porters first sold off goods the *Dash* had transported from Bermuda and Wilmington, North Carolina. Because of the high war prices, the cargo brought in such a profit that the Porters were able to repay their debts and keep the

A Sea Battle for the Ages

On September 5, 1813, during the War of 1812, the British ship HMS *Boxer* and the American USS *Enterprise* battled fiercely off the coast of Monhegan Island forty miles from Portland Harbor. By the time the smoke cleared after less than an hour of fighting, the crew of the *Boxer* had surrendered. The Americans' jubilation was tempered by the fact that both captains died in the firefight. Their remains were carried to Union Wharf, where the remnants of the two ships would also be brought.

The captain of the *Boxer*, Lieutenant Samuel Blyth, 29, had been a seaman since age eleven and was a veteran of the French wars. The *Boxer*, outfitted with sixteen guns and eighty-plus men, had captured three American ships off the coast of Maine in August. The following month, Blyth agreed to escort the American privateer *Margaretta* from St. John, New Brunswick, to Bath, Maine. For his effort, Blyth was paid one hundred pounds. The *Margaretta* sought protection because it carried banned imports from Great Britain. On September 5, as the *Boxer* escorted the *Margaretta* toward the Kennebec River, Blyth fired a few gunshots at the privateer. The captains had previously agreed that the shots be fired, to avoid suspicion in case anyone saw the ships together. A fisherman who heard the shots reported the incident to Lieutenant William Burrows, captain of the USS *Enterprise*, which was anchored off the Maine coast.

Burrows was twenty-eight and had been a seaman for thirteen years. He had sailed aboard the famous "Old Ironsides," where one of his messmates was Henry Wadsworth, uncle of the famous Portland poet, Henry Wadsworth Longfellow. Ignored for promotions previously, he took over the *Enterprise* in 1813 with high hopes. The American vessel was built in 1799 in Baltimore as a 135-ton schooner with twelve guns. In 1812 the *Enterprise* was expanded to 165 tons. The so-called "Lucky Little Enterprise" had captured more prizes than *Old Ironsides*. Though its guns were heavier than those of the *Boxer* and its sides thicker, the American ship was easy to maneuver and speedier than its British counterpart. On that fateful day in 1813, the *Enterprise* had a crew of eighty-three men.

Upon hearing of the shooting by the *Boxer*, Burrows quickly sailed the *Enterprise* until he spied the British ship at 5 a.m. Both ships sat still for three and one-half hours. At 8:30 a.m. the *Boxer* hoisted its flag and fired an opening shot. Burrows declared he would outsail the enemy ship. His dismayed crew protested that they wanted to stay and fight, but the captain headed the *Enterprise* toward the open sea.

A becalmed sea soon stopped both ships dead in the water, where they spent the next six hours sizing each other up. At 3 p.m. the wind finally came up, and the ships pulled within two hundred feet parallel of each other. The *Boxer* fired first, shattering a rail on the American ship. The *Enterprise*'s retaliatory 18-pound shot killed Lieutenant

Blyth instantly, almost cutting him in half. In the ensuing volley of gunfire, a bullet entered Lieutenant Burrows' thigh and coursed through his body, mortally wounding him. "We'll take her yet. Don't haul down the flag," the dying Burrows ordered his crew.

At 3:35 p.m., Lieutenant McCall, who had assumed command of the *Enterprise*, brought the ship across the *Boxer*'s bow. Under incessant American firing, the British ship's topmast and rigging crashed into the sea, forcing the *Boxer* to surrender. Lieutenant McCrery of the *Boxer* brought Blyth's sword to Burrows, who whispered, "I die content." He survived for eight more hours. After Burrows died, his crew wrapped him in an American flag. Burrows was the only American casualty of the day; twenty-five English seamen died in the battle.

Three days later, on September 8, hundreds of people watched as a barge carried the bodies of Burrows and Blyth to Union Wharf. The *Portland Gazette* reported that men, women, and children lined both sides of the street as well as the tops of houses, "anxious to gaze upon this new and interesting spectacle—and solemn silence was kept."

As the *Enterprise* and *Boxer* sailed to the wharf, the Americans guiding them fired guns of salute. At Union Wharf, the captains' twin mahogany coffins, draped with their ships' flags, were transferred onto the town's only real hearse and a makeshift hearse. To the beat of muffled drums, the hearses drove past the respectfully silent crowd to a funeral service at the Second Parish Meeting House on Middle Street. Local officials led those on foot as a full band played mournful music. The clergy came next, followed by the chief mourners—the crew members of the two vessels.

During the funeral, business in the town was suspended and ships in harbor flew their flags at half mast. Following the services, mourners walked to Eastern Cemetery, near the Portland Observatory. After the appropriate military salutes, the bodies were interred side by side, where they remain today. Ironically, the crew of the *Boxer* marked Blyth's grave, but Burrows' grave remained unmarked for two years. In 1815 Matthew Davis, a friend of vice president Aaron Burr, finally paid for a tombstone for Burrows.

The *Enterprise*'s triumph was celebrated throughout the nation. Its victory and other successful U.S. battles at sea proved that American frigates could best the ships of the world's premiere navy. Portland feted the crew of the *Enterprise* with a gala public dinner at Union Hall on Temple Street two days after the funeral. There, Nathaniel Deering, a Union Wharf proprietor, sang an original ode of celebration. A cartoon version of the famous battle showed President James Madison bloodying King George's nose in a prize fight. New Yorkers reworded a drinking tune and sang:

> The gallant *Enterprise* has sail'd and sought
>   the foe, Sirs.
> She met the *Boxer* on the maine
> And brought her home in tow, Sirs!

The badly damaged *Boxer* sat at Union Wharf until Thomas Merrill Jr. bought the vessel at auction for $5,600. Several cannons and thirty-six tons of iron ballast from the *Boxer* fetched an additional $4,175. Burrows' heirs received $1,015 in prize money, and the crew was awarded $55 apiece. After the war, William McLellan Jr. bought the vessel and served as its captain. The McLellans used the ship as a commercial vessel until 1845. Its fate after that is unrecorded.

After a brief stint patrolling the waters off Florida, the *Enterprise* guarded Charleston, South Carolina, for the remainder of the war. In 1823, it was shipwrecked in the West Indies.

One seven-year-old Portlander never forgot the affair. Years later, Henry Wadsworth Longfellow immortalized the battle in one of his best-loved poems, "My Lost Youth":

> I remember the sea-fight far away
> How it thundered o'er the tide!
> And the dead captains, as they lay
> In their graves, o'erlooking the tranquil
>   bay
> Where they in battle died.

Dash. Flour that cost $4 per barrel in Wilmington, for example, sold at $15 per barrel in Portland, while tobacco that cost the merchants three cents per pound sold for three times that amount in Maine.

The *Dash* continued its streak, capturing six British ships in one three-week period. On January 4, 1815, John Porter, Seward Porter's brother, took the *Dash* back out to sea alongside a private schooner, the *Champlain*, to help test the *Champlain*'s speed. On the second day out, the *Champlain* lost sight of the *Dash* as it sped toward Georges Bank. Caught in a gale, the *Dash* disappeared forever along with its twenty-four-year-old captain and sixty sailors. Seward Porter lost John and two other brothers on the voyage.

Before the War of 1812 ended, Union Wharf earned a footnote in history books as the site of a funeral procession for two sea captains killed in a ferocious sea battle off the coast of Monhegan Island. The two captains—one in charge of the USS *Enterprise*, the other commander of Britain's *Boxer*—died September 5, 1813. The Americans won the battle and brought the bodies of the captains to Portland, where they were buried in Eastern Cemetery after ceremonies at Union Wharf and a service at Second Parish Church.

When the British sacked the city later in the war, residents carried kegs of rum stored on Union Wharf to a hideaway in Gorham. "They had one heck of a big party in Gorham," says Parker Poole Jr., who has served as wharfinger since 1964.

During the first two decades of Union Wharf's existence, European navies had looted American merchant ships of their goods and forced their crews into service. U.S. President Jefferson and the U.S. Congress had all but closed down American ports by proclaiming an embargo. A war had endangered the wharf's businesses and interfered with marine trade. Through it all, the Proprietors of Union Wharf managed to pay dividends to its shareholders.

The schooner William Keene, owned by W.H. Shurtleff Company, transported salt from Union Wharf to fishing ports along the Maine coast. The vessel was launched June 2, 1866, at Newcastle, Maine, captained by Joseph Dewyea, who also held a one-eighth share in the ship. S.L. Foster, who held a one-sixteenth share in the boat, built the vessel; J.J. Taylor was master carpenter on the job. The 68-foot-2-inch-long schooner had a beam of 20 feet 2 inches and a draft of 7 feet 5 inches. A crew of two manned the William Keene, which hauled cargo weighing up to 63 tons gross (60 tons net) per trip.

II

Old West Indies Trade

With the end of the War of 1812, the U.S. economy thrived once again. For the next several decades, the Portland waterfront profited from what later became known as the Old West Indies trade. Large, graceful, square-rigged ships sailed the seas between Maine and the West Indies.

The ships, which weighed an average of two hundred tons, brought a variety of products, including grain, vegetables, butter, cheese, meat, and fur to the West Indies and returned to Maine with sugar and molasses. A large part of Maine's exports were shooks (folded-up barrels), used as storage containers for West Indies molasses and sugar.

Most ships made two trips a year, usually leaving Union Wharf at the end of December and arriving in the West Indies islands at the end of the Christmas holidays, then returning home by late February. The second voyage was commonly made in April. Sailors stayed away from the tropics in the summer to avoid the hurricane season and yellow fever and to help plant the crops at home. Sailing was a risky business at any time, though. Seamen braved reefs, gales, and pirates as well as shifting markets.

PIRACY ON THE OPEN SEA

Piracy flourished on the open seas between the sixteenth and the early nineteenth century. Merchant ships, carrying valuable goods and chests full of gold, had no contact with those on land once they began their journey. During their slow passage across the ocean, they had few defenses against the ruthless thieves who roamed the boundless ocean.

Wars and shipboard conditions united to encourage piracy in the 1700s and early 1800s. During the Napoleonic wars, England and France commissioned private sailors to plunder the merchant ships of their enemies. Similar lootings occurred before and during the War of 1812 among French, English, and American sailors. Once the wars were over, a number of unemployed sailors turned to piracy as a way to earn a living. Cruel captains who favored lashing, food shortages, and inhumane working conditions led some sailors to jump ship and join the roving bands of pirates who terrorized ocean travelers.

No Luxury Cruise

Once reputable members of the world of shipping, many men left to become pirates because of the low wages and deplorable on-board conditions they endured as mariners. In the 1700s, some vessels, whose captains were notorious for their brutality, became known as "hell ships." Even without sadistic officers, the journeys promised seasickness, stormy weather, and deprivation. Most of the vessels traveling between Union Wharf and the West Indies were small brigs with low decks. On deck, the crew shared already scant space with ten-foot-high piles of lumber, which often shifted during the less-than-stable crossing. The ship was generally wet and uncomfortable. Even officers had to share their quarters with barrels of potatoes or other freight.

Beginning in the 1700s, England initiated a serious push to end piracy. England's King George I issued a proclamation of amnesty in the first part of the 1700s that allowed pirates who gave up their trade to escape prosecution and to keep their stolen treasure. Those who didn't accept the amnesty faced death if caught. In 1717 England sent Captain Woodes Rogers to the Bahamas, where one thousand pirates had established a base. After a fierce battle, Rogers and his men took over the island and broke up the pirates' operation. Though the raid weakened the pirates' base, individual pirate bands continued to harass merchant ships for another century.

The graves of the two captains of the Boxer and the Enterprise, killed during the War of 1812 and buried in Eastern Cemetery

The aftermath of the Great Fire of 1866, looking up Exchange Street from Fore Street

An 1880s view of Union Wharf from Commercial Street. At right is the Union Wharf office of N.O. Cram.

A certificate of stock in the Proprietors of Union Wharf, worth $2,000. The first certificate was issued on April 3, 1897, to George A. Shurtleff, the brother of W.H. Shurtleff.

View of Commercial Street, 1915. Tracks ran through the center of the street and connected to Union Wharf on the right. The W.H. Shurtleff Company building marked the beginning of Union Wharf.

Sailing ships in Portland Harbor around 1910

The W.H. Shurtleff Company building at the head of Union Wharf in the 1920s. W.H. Shurtleff is peering out the window on the second floor at right.

SHURTLEFF FAMILY LINE

William Shurtleff m. Elizabeth Lettice
1624-1666   1639-1693

William Shurtleff m. Susanna Lothrop
1657-1729   1643-1726

Thomas Shurtleff m. Phebe Shaw
1687-1730   1690-1730

Jonathan Shurtleff m. Elizabeth Leach
1727-after 1783   1727-after 1783

Simeon Shurtleff m. Submit Kingman
1758-1808   1763-1850

Alva Shurtleff m. Anna Shaw
1786-1869   1786-1851

Sylvan Shurtleff m. Martha Jackson
1828-1916   1828-1907

William Henry Shurtleff m. Elizabeth Milliken
1860-1934   1865-1914

Marjorie Clark Shurtleff m. Parker Poole Sr.
1898-1976   1891-1965

Katherine
William Poole m. Dana Smith   Parker Poole Jr. m. Victoria Simes
1923-   1928-   1926-   1927-

Sylvan Shurtleff, c. 1909

W.H. Shurtleff, 1909

POOLE FAMILY LINE

Parker Poole Jr. m. Victoria Simes
1926-   1927-

Malcolm F. Poole	Parker Poole III	Charles A. Poole	Christina C. Poole	Talcott S. Poole	Alexandra Shurtleff Poole
1951-	1952-	1954-	1956-	1958-1982	1964-
m. Ruth Wiggins	m. Susan Mangum	m. Elizabeth Engelke	m. Henry Briscoe Thomas		m. Mark Sawyer
div. 1995					

Malcolm A. Poole	Parker Poole IV	Emily O. Poole	Victoria M. Thomas		Charlotte W. Sawyer
1977-	1987-	1984-	1985-		1994-
Elizabeth F. Poole	Christopher T. Poole	Harold R. Poole	Rebecca P. Thomas		Hannah R. Sawyer
1978-	1989-	1987-	1987-		1997-
Stuart W. Poole	William A. Poole	Jonathan S. Poole	Anne B. Thomas		
1981-	1990-	1989-	1990-		
	Hollister A. Poole				
	1992-				

47

F.J. O'Hara's trawler Notre Dame anchors at the end of Union Wharf on February 27, 1940. O'Hara, a fish processing firm, occupied the east side of the wharf for many years.

Marjorie Shurtleff Poole around 1950. She inherited several shares in the Proprietors of Union Wharf from her father, W.H. Shurtleff. After her father's death, Marjorie's husband, Parker Poole Sr., assumed leadership of the wharf corporation and of W.H. Shurtleff Company.

The Randall and McAllister coal pocket in the 1940s. A fire in 1947 demolished the pocket and put an end to Union Wharf's coal storage business.

Parker Poole Sr. shows off a prize catch outside John Flaherty's fish market on Union Wharf in the late 1950s. An avid fisherman, Poole often brought his catch to Flaherty to be cut and processed. Parker Poole Jr. remembers that the family always ate salmon caught by his father for their Fourth of July feast.

Union Wharf merchants had their own experiences with pirates. In the late 1700s, pirates murdered the crew and burned the brig *Mechanic* after it left Portland on a trade mission. Other Portland vessels had to travel out of their way to avoid pockets of piracy along their route.

At the end of the eighteenth century, the United States passed laws to outlaw piracy, but juries usually failed to convict; too many seamen and their families knew of the appalling conditions aboard merchant ships and the low wages that drew men into the unlawful trade.

In 1815, an outbreak of robberies at sea threatened the shipping trade in the West Atlantic. Sailors discharged from privateer ships active in the War of 1812 were among the pirates conducting the raids. It was the last major threat by pirates, however. Determined to protect their growing marine trade, England and the United States joined forces to eliminate the plague. The combined efforts of the two navies finally managed to exterminate the pirate trade.

HAITI'S ATROCITIES

Haiti's coffee plantations provided Portland merchants with a profitable product that brought high prices back to New England. That trade was irreparably damaged, however, in the early 1790s, when black and mulatto slaves in Haiti revolted against the miserable conditions on the French-owned plantations. In November 1791 the French consul reported that nearly seventy thousand blacks participated in the insurrections that destroyed 172 sugar plantations and 931 coffee plantations. U.S. seamen trading in the West Indies, including those from Union Wharf, witnessed atrocities by blacks, Europeans, and mulattos alike.

The *Cumberland* (Maine) *Gazette* reported incidents observed by Asa Clapp and William McLellan. In November 1791, Clapp arrived in Port Au Prince on the brig *Lion*. Tensions between the French landowners and mulattos had reached fever pitch. Mulattos had hung a Frenchman after the French tried to execute a mulatto. The ruling French officials then demanded that mulattos surrender their arms or leave town. Instead, a group of mulattos marched to the governor's house, where they were met by more than two thousand French soldiers. During the ensuing battle, 100 Frenchmen lost their lives and 150 were jailed. Mulattos set fire to almost every building in town.

In retaliation, the French threatened to execute every black or mulatto in town, and an "indiscriminate slaughter took place," the *Gazette* reported. Captain McLellan, sailing on a different, unnamed vessel, witnessed the same atrocities reported by Clapp. On its return voyage, McLellan's ship encountered a gale during which a crew member drowned and another passenger died in his cabin.

The black population eventually won control of the island nation, but it took decades for Haiti to recover from the devastation caused during the rebellion.

THE WILD WINDS BLOW

Storms posed a serious threat to those who made their livelihood on the sea. The Great Gale of 1830 claimed four of seven vessels that left Portland for the Caribbean during three days in early December. A fifth ship limped into port five weeks late. William McLellan Jr.'s brig *Hind* was among those caught in the storm. The *Hind* was bound for Cuba with lumber, scheduled to return with molasses, when the storm hit three days out. For sixty-six days the Portland sailing community heard nothing about the *Hind.* Then it was reported that a Boston-based ship had found the wreck of the *Hind* full of water, with no masts. A jug of water, a mattress, pieces of beef, a pair of mittens, and a makeshift hut of rough boards testified to the attempts of the crew to survive. The only clue to the crew's fate was a message cut into the deck with a sailor's knife: "McLellan master, P. Hall, mate Dec 7, lat 39 30 N, lon 67 50 W."

Unbeknown to family and friends waiting anxiously for word of their loved ones, the *Hind*'s crew had been picked up nine days after the storm by the *Charles Carroll* out of Newburyport, four hundred miles adrift of their stated position. With no telegraphs yet, the news of their rescue did not arrive in Portland until the sailors did. McLellan and his crew survived the storm by tying themselves to the deck fittings or holding onto wreckage, huddling behind the remains of the bulwark.

By the age of 30, McLellan had amassed a fortune. He later retired to a luxurious Portland house, where he lived comfortably until his death in 1844.

Dangerous though the sea could be, it continued to be the anchor for the thriving Portland economy. By 1832, Portland boasted the largest commercial fleet on the East Coast. It monopolized the shook trade and was the largest molasses importer next to Boston. The harbor streets bustled with singing stevedores unloading cargoes, sailors from faraway ports out for a night on the town, and ox teams hauling lumber and other goods from the surrounding forests. Poet Henry Wadsworth Longfellow, born in Portland in 1807, immortalized this time in "My Lost Youth":

> I remember the black wharves and the slips,
> And the sea-tides tossing free;
> And Spanish sailors with bearded lips,
> And the beauty and mystery of the ships,
> And the magic of the sea . . .

TENANTS AND TRADE

Union Wharf and neighboring Widgery's Wharf remained a center for the rum and molasses trade. Merchant J. B. Brown, who along with partner St. John Smith rented space on Union Wharf in 1837 and 1840, discovered how to make brown sugar from molasses and established the Portland Sugar House in 1855 on Commercial Street. The business employed 150 workers and produced three hundred barrels of sugar a day. Jacob McLellan was one of five directors of the Sugar House.

Union Wharf's tenants during this period represented a wide range of craftsmen, many of whom worked in the marine trades. They included blacksmith John Averill, sail maker William Bartlett, riggers David Boyd and James Wylie, block and pump maker Levi Bryant, coopers Jabez Clapp and Luther Flood, and boat builders Thomas Roberts and Joseph Roberts.

The Farmer's Magazine (a storage firm) typified large businesses on Union Wharf at the time. In 1837, the company entered a ten-year lease for a three-hundred-foot-long lot on the southeast end of the dock to store and sell hay and other goods. The firm erected a wooden, two-story storehouse, with a round, shingled roof. Running 250 feet long and 42 feet wide, the structure contained a 12-foot passageway through the middle. The terms of the lease also required the company's agent, Joshua Cross, to leave a passageway on each side of his lot—"said platform to be well built and planked and kept in good repair." Like other lessees, Cross was allowed free dockage for all goods not shipped out by water, and hay could be shipped free of dockage, though other goods were subject to the prevailing rates. As was the custom, Cross paid the taxes on the building while the Proprietors of Union Wharf paid those on the wharf itself. The Magazine's rent was $327.75 per year. The Proprietors noted, as they did with all tenants, that they were not responsible for any "extraordinary casualty" to the building or damage from the settling of the sea under the wharf or "braking in of the sea" into the building.

As business boomed, the Proprietors of Union Wharf continued to revise their rules and rates, distributing 150 copies of the 1823 rulebook to current and prospective tenants. In 1838, they voted to adopt the same rates and rules as those on Long Wharf, except regarding plaster and wood bark, and printed two hundred copies of the new rulebook. A decade later the Proprietors again revised rates after they consulted with other wharf owners. At this time, Union Wharf discontinued its practice of allowing store tenants to land goods on the rear side of their stores for free. Instead, the Proprietors charged one fee for all merchandise imported or exported from the wharf, except that if the merchandise remained with the owner and did not leave the store, it could be reshipped later without charge.

Other rules noted that no mahogany, timber, or lumber could lie on the wharf longer than ten days without the wharfinger's consent, and no masts or spars could be stored there for more than a week. Lumber could not be piled within twelve feet of any store.

The list of products in the 1848 wharfage ratebook illustrates the diversity of goods moving across the wharf. It included foodstuffs such as lemons, cabbages, salt, and tea; candles, carpets, and other household supplies; goods such as cotton, hemp, and rags; and cigars and goat skins.

A Bigger, Better Wharf

During Union Wharf's first fifty years, the Proprietors made continuous expansions and physical improvements. In 1810 they added nearly 400 feet to the length of the wharf, which with the new addition extended 2,200 feet from Fore Street into the bay. In 1824 they authorized the building of a stone wall 100 feet by 25 feet back to the jog (the projecting part of the pier). Twelve years later, the storeowners whose buildings were located on the "first block" of the wharf (nearest land) had to raise their buildings so the wharfinger, Samuel Ilsley, could lay a sidewalk in front of the stores. In 1842, the wharf owners voted to build a dolphin, or resting place for ships. Apparently, a small fence on the wharf's east side had been built, because records show that in 1849 it was repaired. Workers cleared ice off the docks as part of their regular maintenance work.

The wharfinger generally oversaw the day-to-day operations of the wharf. A Wharf Committee of three, elected from among the shareholders, involved themselves in such matters as determining boundary lines, setting rates, and helping to settle lawsuits. Usually the wharfinger and Wharf Committee members served for a number of years. For example, Samuel Hussey served as wharfinger from 1816 to 1826 and as clerk in 1820, while Hezekiah Winslow served as wharfinger for four years beginning in 1827.

The makeup of the Proprietors shifted gradually as the original shareholders died and heirs took their place. In 1844, the heirs of Abel Jones, with five shares, had become the largest shareholders. Heirs of Ralph Cross, wharfinger Robert Boyd, and Andrew Emerson also held shares in the wharf during this period, as did the McLellans and the Jewetts.

THE HORNED HOG

The 1820s brought a new kind of vessel to Union Wharf: the passenger steamboat. These flat-bottomed boats were powered by steam and featured distinctive paddle wheels on the side of the vessel—prompting the nickname "sidewheelers." Captain Seward Porter, Union Wharf merchant and owner of the famed *Dash* privateer, launched Maine's first successful steamer, the *Kennebec*, in 1822 on the Kennebec River. The river currents proved too strong for the vessel, however, so Porter moved the boat to Union Wharf to be run to the nearby islands on a seasonal basis. The small, flat-bottomed boat with a sharp prow and raked sides earned the derisive nickname "Horned Hog." Porter had the last laugh, though, as his new-fangled steamboat powered across the bay past other vessels becalmed by the still air.

The *Kennebec* was far from reliable, however. During strong northwest winds, the *Kennebec* had to stay at Peaks Island until the wind shifted. The boat's engine stalled five or six times each trip, and all hands, including passengers, had to turn the paddle wheels by hand to keep the boat going.

Porter ran the *Kennebec* irregularly. A notice in the *Eastern Argus* newspaper of August 13, 1822, announced that tickets for a trip aboard the *Kennebec* were on sale at A.W. Tinkham's store. The boat was scheduled to leave Union Wharf at 4 a.m. to spend the day in North Yarmouth. A side trip to North Yarmouth Academy's commencement exercises was also offered if enough passengers were interested.

Portland constable Lewis Pease's couplet extolled the *Kennebec*'s virtues:

> A fig for all your clumsy craft
> Your pleasure boats and packets
> The steamboat lands you safe and soon
> At Mansfield's, Trott's, or Brackett's.

Porter also brought the steamer *Connecticut*, which had been launched on Long Island Sound in 1816, to Casco Bay in 1823. Porter put the *Connecticut* into service as a passenger boat between Union Wharf and Boston. The boat made about one trip a week.

In March 1834 the Proprietors voted that the steamboats *Connecticut*, *Chancellor*, and *Livingston* would be required to pay dockage at a monthly rate to be determined. These initial short trips heralded the arrival of regular Portland-to-Liverpool steamship service later in the century.

With steamers and masted ships of every description lining up at its docks, Union Wharf was at the hub of transportation and trade in Portland and the state. In 1846 it was one of thirteen wharves in the city that together handled 28,014 tons of imports and 45,906 tons of exports.

Dozens of stores set up shop on Fish Lane (today's Exchange Street) and nearby streets to handle the merchandise flowing through Portland's port. The area quickly became a prosperous mercantile center. A group of the city's wealthy merchants were among those who paid to dig a canal from Casco Bay to Sebago Lake to encourage Maine businesses in the center of the state to ship their products to the waterfront market. But by the time the Cumberland and Oxford Canal was finished in 1830, a new form of transportation was set to enter the picture, the railroad. Its introduction to Portland would alter the physical face of the harbor and change the marine trade business forever.

III

Rise of the Railroad

As prosperous as the first half of the nineteenth century had been for Union Wharf and the city of Portland, calamity and change marked the last half of the 1800s.

Perhaps the biggest change revolved around the construction of railroads in Portland. Portland lawyer and community leader John Alfred Poor spearheaded the effort to extend Canada's Grand Trunk Railway from Montreal to Portland in the 1840s and 1850s. Poor, a leader in the newly organized Portland Board of Trade, had traveled from Portland to Montreal aboard a sleigh in the winter of 1845. His quick journey proved to Canadian farmers that a railroad along the same route would provide a rapid way to get their wheat to market during the winter when the St. Lawrence River froze over. Poor touted his city's natural advantages: Portland Harbor remained ice-free, it was a half-day closer to Liverpool than Boston or New York, and it possessed a deep entrance, nine miles of frontage, and shelter from storms.

If the city was to lure the Canadian trade to Portland, it had to develop a distribution system that would link the Canadian Grand Trunk Railway to Maine railroads and to Portland's docks. To accomplish this, Portland's leaders agreed to build a road with tracks down its center that ran parallel to the docks at the high-tide mark. The building of Commercial Street, one hundred feet wide and nearly a mile long, was the most significant physical transformation of the waterfront area since its development in the 1600s. It required builders to fill in the bay area below Fore Street and to construct a road right through the middle of the existing wharves, including Union Wharf. Completed in 1853, Commercial Street changed the face of the waterfront. Businesses that had once been dockside now had a street between them and the water. Others lost their lots completely to the new road. The city paid damages to those businesses that had to relocate.

Union Wharf, once extending 2,200 feet into the harbor, was reduced to 1,100 feet on the waterside, with the rest of its property landlocked to the west of Commercial Street. The Proprietors voted to reassign new lots on the wharf to those whose lots had been taken. The Proprietors also attempted to sell their land on the west side of Commercial Street. In the summer of 1851, they voted to sell, at a price of at least $40 a foot, lots to anyone willing to erect a brick or stone store within two years. They also offered to sell the whole section for $10,000 to any company that would build a line of stores within a year, as long as all the storeowners occupying the property agreed to exchange their lots for ones on the wharf.

The disruption caused by the building of Commercial Street made it difficult for the Proprietors to sell their landside lots or to find profitable tenants. In 1852 they voted to allow businesses to build on vacant lots on the wharf for free as long as they paid wharfage on goods transported by water. The following year the Proprietors auctioned off the northwest corner of the lot across Commercial Street, and in 1856 they agreed to sell the upper east end, both to expedite the laying of railroad tracks and to "liquidate [their] debts."

The new era of rail transportation had arrived. The Atlantic & St. Lawrence Railroad, constructed at the east end of the waterfront in 1853, leased its property to Canada's Grand Trunk Railway. Tracks running the length of Commercial Street connected the Canadian railway to Maine railroads. Trains sped along Commercial Street, belching smoke and carrying goods to and from the docks.

The wharves, split in half by the new street, scrambled to take advantage of the opportunities the railroads brought to the waterfront. The Proprietors of Union Wharf built a connecting track down the middle of the wharf in 1856 and another one down the rear of the buildings in 1859. In 1862 they joined other wharves in setting standard wharfage fees for goods brought by railroad. The Proprietors took other action to protect their wharf property from fire. In 1852 they prohibited the construction of wooden buildings on the wharf higher than fifteen feet, or twenty-six feet if the structure had a tin roof. They also allocated $250 to entice the owners of four vacant lots on the wharf to build "fireproof" structures.

THE PROPRIETORS INCORPORATE

Despite the major upheaval along the waterfront, the Proprietors posted a dividend of $40 in 1856. However, as the global marketplace grew and technology progressed, business transactions became more complicated. Perhaps spurred by a desire to protect themselves from increasing financial and legal risks, the Proprietors decided to incorporate their business.

On February 9, 1856, the Maine Legislature approved a charter of incorporation for the Proprietors of Union Wharf. The terms of incorporation gave the Proprietors of Union Wharf control over the wharf and its operation. Individual businesses owned or rented lots on the wharf. Among those businesses, many were owned and operated by the shareholders of the Proprietors of Union Wharf. The corporation had the final say on the type of business allowed on the wharf, the construction of buildings, and other matters. Under the new charter, the corporation was responsible for taxes on the wharf itself; businesses on the wharf had to pay taxes on their own buildings. The twenty-eight shares owned by individual proprietors were considered personal, not corporate, property.

The corporation's bylaws, adopted in 1856, provided for an annual meeting to choose a standing committee of three to examine all accounts, advise and direct the wharfinger, and adjust and settle any disputes. The bylaws added the office of president to the existing positions of wharfinger, clerk, and treasurer. With the exception of 1876, a single person held all three of the latter posts. The majority of officers served continuously for years, providing stability to the wharf operations. Over the years, control of the wharf passed through several generations of the same families, from the McLellans in the late 1700s to the mid 1800s to the Shurtleffs, who began service in the late 1850s and whose descendants own the wharf today.

Amendments approved in 1866 fixed the capital stock at $56,000. A further provision stipulated that assessments up to $1,000 could be made on each share for repairs and improvements to the property. The Proprietors also voted to sell all the property they owned in common to the corporation.

Once the difficulties from the construction of Commercial Street were past, Union Wharf and the waterfront prospered again. John Poor's vision of making Portland Canada's winter port came to fruition as Canadian grain rode the rails straight to Portland's wharves. It would become the port's most important export by the turn of the century. Fish, leather, cordwood, and other goods crossed Portland's docks on the way to market. The Board of Trade, established in 1853, targeted port development as one of its first goals and helped get funding to mark and light the harbor, develop frontage lines along the wharves (including at Union Wharf in 1868), and dredge the channels to make them deeper.

Shipping and shipbuilding continued to play a central role in the port's economy. In 1855, Portland and its environs were seventh in the nation in the tons of ships constructed. Between 1794 and 1860, shipping registered in Portland rose from fourteen thousand tons to more than eighty-one thousand tons.

Prohibition Tests Trade

In the early part of the nineteenth century, much of the molasses imported from the West Indies went to produce rum. Several distilleries rented space on Union Wharf during that time. Rum was an everyday beverage for Mainers; workers stopped for rum rather than coffee breaks.

Public drunkenness, fights, alcohol-related accidents, and families left destitute because of alcoholism prompted a group of Maine citizens, led by Neal Dow, to seek restrictions on liquor. Responding to the pleas of the Maine Temperance Union and its supporters, the state Legislature passed the first anti-liquor law in the United States in 1841. Maine again led the nation in the push for prohibition when it passed a statewide ban on the sale of alcohol except for industrial or medical uses in 1851. Within four years, twelve other states had adopted similar measures.

The port's major business still revolved around wood and molasses in 1858. Wood accounted for 78 percent of the port's exports, and molasses and sugar made up 71 percent of imports. In 1860 Portland was the second largest molasses port in the country. Six million gallons of the sweet syrup passed through the port annually. Union Wharf contained one molasses shed; neighboring Widgery's Wharf had two large ones. Ships docking at Union and Widgery's sat two to three abreast waiting for space. Onlookers described the area as a "forest of masts and spars."

The state prohibition closed down Portland's rum distilleries and put a damper on the molasses trade. Those trading in liquor had to do so in secret. Merchants, manufacturers, and ordinary citizens objected to the ban on alcohol, and many ignored the law. In 1856, Maine repealed the ban and replaced it with a law requiring sellers and manufacturers to be licensed. Undeterred, the prohibitionists—united nationally under the National Prohibition Party—continued their efforts to ban alcohol. Maine passed a new, though weaker, prohibition law in 1858. Distillers and others involved in the rum trade fought against the ban throughout the end of the century and into the next. In 1884, the state Legislature, with a push from Dow, adopted prohibition as part of the Maine constitution. The passage of the Eighteenth Amendment to the U.S. Constitution in 1919 established Prohibition on the national level. It was later repealed by the Twenty-first Amendment, adopted in 1933.

CIVIL WAR

As the United States headed into the second half of the century, cataclysmic forces threatened the nation's existence. Portland's poet, Henry Wadsworth Longfellow, referred to the danger his country faced in "The Building of the Ship," published in 1851. It was said that President Lincoln's eyes filled with tears and he could not speak when he first heard the poem recited. It ends with a stirring verse in which the poet expressed his fears for the country as it faced the perils ahead:

Civil War Comes to Union Wharf

During the Civil War, a Union Wharf clerk became a soldier for a day and helped defeat the Confederates in a skirmish in Portland Harbor. James Brackett, an office clerk at Fillebrown & Burton, flour dealers at the head of Union Wharf, arrived for work on the morning of June 27, 1863. The office was abuzz with reports that a U.S. cutter, the *Caleb Cushing*, had gone to sea without orders. All but one of the vessel's officers were on shore because of the death of their captain. The city was filled with excitement as various reasons for the cutter's disappearance circulated. Some thought the officer left in charge, a Georgia native, had seized the cutter on behalf of the Confederates. Word then came that Mr. Jewett, the collector of the port, had dispatched the towboat, *Tiger*, and the *Forest City* steamer from Boston to pursue the cutter. News followed that Mayor Jacob McLellan, "with his usual push and energy," had chartered the New York-based steamer *Chesapeake* to join the chase.

"The neighboring merchants and clerks all visited the scene of the activities, each bringing back new and exciting reports," Brackett wrote. "I chafed considerably at my confinement in the store." The proprietors of Fillebrown & Burton took turns checking out the activity, and Brackett feared his turn would come too late. Finally, he was allowed to leave. Brackett had been turned down for military service several times. He decided that he would join the call for volunteers if needed, even if it meant losing his job. As he ran down the wharf, he heard Mayor McLellan cry, "This the last [musket], who takes it?" Brackett jumped for it and boarded the *Chesapeake.*

The *Chesapeake,* normally a passenger steamboat, was armed only with muskets. Charles Knapp, shipmaster of the port, and Mr. Harris, a hat store owner, co-captained the vessel. The *Caleb Cushing,* a topsail rigger, sported a heavy gun that could be swung in any direction. Brackett tucked his musket in his waistband and positioned himself behind one of the cotton bales put up around the vessel as protection.

The *Chesapeake* soon caught up with the *Forest City,* which was "popping away" long range at the *Caleb Cushing.* Deciding its exposed paddlewheels made the *Forest City* too vulnerable, the steamer's captain retreated, leaving the *Chesapeake* to fight alone. The *Chesapeake* steamed toward the cutter. The *Caleb Cushing* in turn fired at the *Chesapeake.* It missed, but it headed full steam toward the *Chesapeake.* "It looked like it was going to be something more than a picnic," Brackett observed later. Brackett and his mates didn't know that the cutter had only loose gunpowder left as ammunition.

The *Chesapeake's* captain ordered the crew to prepare to board the cutter. Brackett wondered how he would jump from a high-deck steamer to a low-deck ship with an ungainly musket, without breaking his neck or falling overboard. Suddenly, smoke began to rise from the hull of the

Caleb Cushing. The cutter's crew had set it on fire and was escaping in rowboats. Spotting the crew, *Chesapeake* captain Charles Knapp yelled, "Fire, boys, fire! They are going to board us!" With that, the cutter's crew put their hands above their heads and shouted, "Don't fire! Don't fire!" Taking charge, Colonel Mason of the Seventh Maine Regiment ordered the *Chesapeake*'s crew to stand down, shouting, "The first man who fires I will run through him."

The *Forest City* picked up the Confederate sympathizers in their rowboats. A disappointed Brackett noted later, "The *Chesapeake* took all the risk, while the Boston steamer [*Forest City*] captured the prize."

Minutes later, the *Caleb Cushing* exploded. Brackett saw "pencils of bright light . . . the vessel broken into innumerable fragments, the whole mass pausing a moment in mid-air, then dropping with a crash into the water."

Brackett and his mates reached Portland around 4 o'clock and were "welcomed by the firing of guns, ringing of bells and the shout of the crowd who covered the wharves and sheds." The victors were treated to a dinner at Barnum's Restaurant on Temple Street, probably in lieu of prize money.

James Brackett came from the Brackett family of Peaks Island, direct descendants of one of the first two settlers in Portland. He later enlisted in the Army of the Potomac and then signed on as a member of the First Maine Cavalry. After the war he returned to Peaks Island where he operated the popular amusement area, Greenwood Gardens. He died in 1926 at 87 years old, leaving no near relations.

Thou, too, sail on, O Ship of State!
Sail on, O *Union,* strong and great!
Humanity with all its fears,
With all the hopes of future years,
Is hanging breathless on thy fate!

Resentment between the northern and southern states that had been seething just below the surface for years finally erupted into a civil war in 1861. Once Fort Sumter fell, Portland and the rest of the state rallied behind the Union. Governor Israel Washburn declared, "The issue involved [union] is one on which there can be no divided opinion in Maine. It affects not only the integrity of the union but the life of Republican government. For the preservation of these, Maine will pour out her best blood." Maine did indeed make the ultimate sacrifice. The state contributed more soldiers to the war than any other in proportion to its population. More than 73,000 Mainers fought for the Union cause, and 8,800 died.

Portland sent 3,636 men to war in five volunteer militias. Uniformed men filled the streets. Home Guards kept a watch out for Confederate privateers at coastal forts, including Fort Scammel, Fort Preble, and Fort Gorges in the Portland area.

For Portland's shippers, the Civil War resulted in both losses and benefits. Confederate raiders at sea drove northern shippers away from their normal routes. The war was particularly disruptive of the West Indies trade, which required traveling southward. Because of the threat of attack, Portland shippers sent only one-fourth of their vessels to the West Indies. They diverted the rest of the fleet to Canada, where a new trade partnership blossomed.

After the war, the West Indies trade never recovered its prominence among Portland's merchants. Surprisingly, though, the war had little lasting effect on trade overall in Portland. After a dip in business at the beginning of the war, trade resumed and exceeded its previous records. Exports rose from $3 million in 1860 to $8.2 million in 1865, and imports rose from $1.4 million to $7.2 million in the same period.

Maine's fleet didn't fare as well. Confederates sank fifty-five Maine ships. Most of the reduction in the fleet came, however, not at the hands of enemy ships but because shipowners could not afford the exorbitantly expensive war insurance on their vessels. Many Maine merchants sold their boats below market value to foreign countries or converted their ships to foreign registration. Between 1860 and 1865, the Maine fleet was reduced by more than three hundred thousand tons.

SHIFTING TRADE WINDS

As the nation struggled to recover from the devastation of the Civil War, Portland faced a disaster of its own. The Great Fire of 1866 swept through the city, burning everything in its path. Only the wharf area was spared. When the flames finally died out, twelve thousand residents were left homeless and fifteen hundred buildings had been destroyed.

In less than a month, the city was well on its way to rebuilding. Two years later, Portland took pride in its new, modern look. A rebuilt Commercial Street bustled with ship brokerage offices, chandleries, food commission brokerage houses, and wholesale grocers. By the 1870s, sixty-five trains a day carried freight and passengers in and out of Portland.

The Great Fire of 1866

By sheer luck, Union Wharf and the other piers escaped the Great Fire of 1866 that destroyed two-thirds of Portland. The fire began on the Fourth of July when someone threw a firecracker near High and Commercial streets, less than a quarter of a mile from Union Wharf. Local men managed to put that fire out, but the wind blew cinders across the street to the roofs of the Portland Sugar House and a foundry.

A gust of wind ignited the cinders, and the fast-moving fire became a blazing wall of flame. Block by block, the city's buildings succumbed to the inferno. Burning cinders and wood blackened the sky and spread the blaze to North Street on Munjoy Hill, more than a mile from the Sugar House, and as far north as Falmouth, five miles away. The fire tore through the busiest and richest parts of the city on a diagonal path, sparing only the wharves downtown. Buildings that had survived the burning of 1775 succumbed to the blaze. Walls crashed into rubble, buildings exploded, spires and cornices tumbled to the ground. The intense heat melted brick, wood, even iron shutters, in an instant. The supposedly fireproof Custom House, built of the finest Quincy granite, resembled flaked limestone, its cornices fallen to the street.

The Fox Building, used to store tools for shipment to the Caribbean, was one of the few buildings spared during the blaze. The owners of the building, at the corner of Exchange and Fore streets, had three ships in port at the time and ordered their crews to form a bucket brigade to keep the brick structure wet.

People fled for their lives, trying to move their families, goods, and furniture to safe places. Many ran to the wharves to escape the blaze. Sprawling on logs or docks or wherever they could, exhausted and disheveled, they clutched whatever possessions they had saved. Employees and store owners worked frantically to save their stock, desperately packing products in carts and boxes and hauling them to the waterfront.

Miraculously, only two people died. There were plenty of close calls, though. One account tells of a forgotten drunk who safely slept in his jail cell through the whole episode as flames reduced his surroundings to ashes. Claims agent Z.K. Harmon, trapped in the Custom House, tried to subdue the flames in the building's upper stories. Finally, with smoke filling every room, he donned several mail bags to protect himself from the flames and ran a gauntlet of fire to escape.

By the time the fire subsided fifteen hours later, it had burned more than two hundred acres and destroyed fifty-eight streets and fifteen hundred buildings. More than one hundred manufacturing plants were demolished, and twelve thousand residents—one-third of the city's population—were left homeless. Most lived in tent cities on Munjoy Hill during the summer as builders erected new homes, office buildings, and other structures.

The city rebuilt in impressive time. With little dispute, insurers quickly paid more than $3 million in insurance claims. The U.S. Congress and the cities of Boston and New York provided financial aid to Portland. In less than a month, the construction of three hundred houses and stores was under way. By August 14, the number of rations handed out to the needy had decreased from 7,200 to 500 a day. Within two years, new parks, schools, churches, and modern buildings lined city streets. An article in the *Boston Journal* noted, "The fire has put Portland fifty years ahead."

Some historians believe, however, that the fire left psychological wounds on the city that stunted its economic and cultural growth through the turn of the century. With the burning of the Sugar House, the Great Fire provided one more nail in the coffin for the molasses trade, which was already in decline. After the fire, the hub of the city shifted from the waterfront to a newly constructed retail and office district several streets inland from the piers.

Union Wharf just barely escaped the devastation of the fire. Nearby Union Street and the north side of Commercial Street completely burned. Two men associated with Union Wharf were among those who suffered the largest losses of the fire. A.K. Shurtleff, who first became affiliated with Union Wharf in 1858, received $400,000 in insurance payments for the destruction of his shoe store, A & S Shurtleff, on Middle Street. Sugar House owner J.B. Brown, who with his partner St. John Smith rented office space on Union Wharf, lost more than a quarter of a million dollars in the destruction of the Sugar House. Both Shurtleff and Brown were savvy businessmen, however, and used the crisis as an opportunity to grow.

Shurtleff abandoned the retail trade for a successful career in shoe manufacturing. Brown played a major role in rebuilding the city. He erected the ornate Falmouth Hotel on Middle Street in 1868 and financed the construction of two other large buildings. The building on Commercial Street between Oak and Casco streets, designed by renowned architect John Calvin Stephens, was finished after Brown's death in 1881 and christened the J.B. Brown block in his memory. Though Brown rebuilt the Sugar House, he eventually closed the business when competitors adopted new technology to transform molasses into sugar that quickly replaced the outdated steam process Brown used. When he died, Brown was the city's largest landowner.

The Proprietors of Union Wharf shared in the prosperity and extended their good fortune to the wharfingers who ran the wharf. They voted to pay wharfingers 5 percent of the annual rents collected from wharf businesses and 15 percent of docking fees beginning in 1880. That wasn't enough, however, for N.O. Cram, who began his term as wharfinger in 1880. He demanded more money. The Proprietors turned him down but later suspected he took the money anyway by embezzling funds from the wharf account. They based their suspicions on Cram's report that the corporation was in debt and had no money to pay a dividend. An inspection of the accounts, however, showed that the corporation was not insolvent. When confronted with the charges at a meeting, Cram refused to resign. In January 1884 the Proprietors voted to remove him, acting under its power "to remove unfaithful agents whenever their [Proprietors'] welfare demands it." It was the first and only time a wharfinger was forced to resign against his will.

Heading off another dispute, the Proprietors took action to prevent nontenants from using the wharf's railroad tracks. In 1881, they instructed the railroads not to direct railcars onto Union Wharf unless they had business there.

The tracks got plenty of use from tenants. Trade with the West Indies continued into the 1880s, with hogsheads, shooks, fish, and lumber being exported in exchange for molasses and sugar. Hogsheads, a type of barrel, and shooks were used as containers for the incoming sugar and molasses. Mills to produce these containers employed many people throughout southern Maine. In 1886, eleven lots on the west side of Union Wharf served as storage areas for shooks alone. Hogsheads filled with molasses lined the cobblestone streets leading to the docks.

But by the end of the century, the molasses trade was on its last legs. Even though the prohibitionists ultimately failed in their attempts to ban alcohol, their temporary successes in restricting its sale and production hampered the molasses and rum trade. Portland's molasses merchants suffered another setback when other countries began shipping the syrup in bulk and sugar in bags, eliminating the need for shooks and hogsheads.

Even as the port's molasses trade dwindled, exports and imports of other products continued, including lumber, fish,

The Shurtleff Connection

Alva (A.K.) Shurtleff's name first appears in the Union Wharf record books in 1858 as a member of the Wharf Committee. Thus began the Shurtleff family's involvement in the affairs of Union Wharf that continues today, five generations later.

In the early 1800s the Shurtleff family, direct descendants of John Alden of Plymouth Colony, settled in Paris, Maine. Alva's brother, Sylvan, was born in 1828, the next to youngest of the family's ten children. He went on to distinguish himself in the world, gaining fame as a custom boot and shoe maker whose trademark became known countrywide. Sylvan was a forward-thinking entrepreneur who used the most up-to-date labor-saving devices in manufacturing. That outlook applied to his home, too, where he gained a small measure of fame as the second person in Portland to light a gas jet.

By 1865 Sylvan had shoe factories in Portland and South Paris that employed four hundred to five hundred workers. He and Alva ran a shoe store, A & S Shurtleff, on Fore Street in Portland. After the Great Fire of 1866 destroyed the store, Sylvan concentrated on manufacturing only. He relocated several times before finally moving the operation to Union Wharf, where the Shurtleff Company would remain until 1964.

The Shurtleffs became a major force on Union Wharf, eventually occupying twelve buildings and holding leadership positions in the wharf corporation. Alva Shurtleff served as a wharfinger from 1870–1873 as well as a member of the Wharf Committee. Sylvan, too, became a proprietor in the corporation.

Alva died in 1879. Sylvan survived to the age of 88, outliving all his siblings. The year before his death in 1915, he sent a note with his renewal order to the *Oxford* (County) *Democrat*, commenting on the changes he had seen in Portland. When he moved his family to Portland sixty-three years before, Commercial Street had not existed. "The great change since that time is wonderful," he said, adding, "I am unable to realize that I am old. My handwriting remains [the] same as when I was 30." When he died the next year, his obituary noted that he was one of the oldest residents of the city, and that such longevity was a Shurtleff characteristic.

Sylvan's sons, George A. and William Henry (W.H.), continued the family's association with Union Wharf. Both owned stock and held long-term positions in the Proprietors of Union Wharf, George as treasurer and William as president. William, born in 1860, began working with his father at the age of 19 and picked up his shrewd business skills. Seeing the need for a distribution center for canned goods, smoked fish, and molasses, William expanded his father's Union Wharf business in 1890 and changed the company's name when it was incorporated as W.H. Shurtleff Company in 1902. By 1900, the company was also importing salt from Turks Island in the West Indies. In 1926,

Shurtleff established a warehouse in Bangor and operated two schooners, the *William Keene* and the *Grace and Alice*, which delivered salt along the Maine coast. The firm entered the industrial chemical field in the 1950s, and today is one of the largest chemical handlers in the region.

William's grandson, William Poole, remembered his grandfather as "very much a gentleman . . . (and a man) who loved to play golf." Parker Poole Jr., another grandson, recalled that the old man, all decked out in a suit and spats, frequently walked up and down the wharf, surveying the activity on the dock.

William Shurtleff's brother, George, served as treasurer of the W.H. Shurtleff Company for many years. He died two days before a 1932 fire extensively damaged the roof and top floors of the firm's offices on Union Wharf. By then, William was in poor health and unable to conduct business. When he died in 1934, his obituary noted that the Shurtleff family had been identified with the salt and cured fish trade for nearly eighty years.

and foodstuffs. Union Wharf in the 1880s was home to dealers in lumber (William H. Walker), corn (A.D. Whidden), wholesale fish and oysters (J. Freeman & Co.), and flour and grain (N.B. Noble & Son). Commission merchants, who brokered the shipping of products, occupied several offices on the wharf. Two of the largest businesses were F.A. Waldron and D.L. Fernald & Company. Waldron, established in 1858, operated a three-story grain, flour, and feed store that measured one hundred feet by five hundred feet and occupied three lots.

D.L. Fernald ran a fish packing and inspecting business from two buildings, both two-story, at the end of the wharf. The British consulate also rented space at Union Wharf during the 1890s.

As the wharf approached its centennial year, new challenges arose. Laws passed after the Civil War that required U.S. merchants to use American-made vessels had reduced the number of ships available for marine trade. Many shippers had switched from marine transportation to the much-faster railroad. Portland's export business took another dive when the Argentinian Republic—one of the port's major buyers of timber—began to cut its own trees.

Union Wharf's list of tenants in 1899 shows the declining importance of exporting at that time. Nine offices were used strictly for storage by nonmaritime businesses, including a mason supplier (Cox & Wood), a carriage woodworker (D.H. Foster), an agricultural and bike dealer (Isaiah Frye), and a "junk" specialist (Thomas Towle).

Union Wharf wasn't open to every business, however. The Proprietors retained control over the types of businesses allowed on the wharf. Fearful of fire, they refused to store petroleum on the wharf in 1883. The year before, the Proprietors spent $4,000 on fire insurance on four salt storage areas and $1,000 on a new shed.

COAL AND SALT

Countering the downward trend in export business, the Proprietors of Union Wharf cultivated two new sources of profit in the 1880s that would continue into the twentieth century—coal and salt. Emery & Furbish erected a salt storehouse on the southwest corner of the wharf, sixty-five feet wide by one hundred feet long and twenty-one feet high, where the firm stored tons of salt shipped mainly from Turks Island in the West Indies. The company held a ten-year lease at $1,500 per year. Local fishermen, residents, and businesses throughout the region bought the salt to preserve and season foods. Other salt stores quickly opened along the wharf to take advantage of the last vestige of the West Indies trade.

The Proprietors also erected a coal shed next door to Emery & Furbish. Coal had been introduced as a fuel for stoves and lighting, and many Maine residents were eager to modernize their homes. The first shipment of coal from Pennsylvania arrived at Widgery's Wharf next to Union around 1830. The Portland Gas Light Company, organized in 1849, was one of the first coal-fueled lighting companies in the United States. On Union Wharf, a similar company, Consolidated Electric Light Company, leased several lots in the 1890s to store coal. By the end of the century Consolidated's storehouse was considered unsafe by the Proprietors, and the firm agreed to make repairs. Two other coal dealers soon located on Union, the J.G. White Coal Company and D.S. Warren.

To accommodate the new tenants and improve the property, the Proprietors made several changes to the wharf. In 1890, they paved two hundred feet of roadway leading down the wharf with granite and made provisions for the laying of pipes. They also signed an agreement with the owners of Merrill's Wharf, on the west side of Union, that set the property line of each structure and guaranteed that neither wharf owner would build any extensions that would obstruct the pas-

The Salt Report

Sales agents from England arranged many of W.H. Shurtleff Company's salt shipments from Spain, Italy, and the West Indies. A 1933 "Salt Report" from Judge & Son, a London firm that sold salt and chartered agents for salt cargoes, lists the origination points and types of salt contained in a number of Shurtleff shipments. Shurtleff usually obtained its product from Torrevieja, Italy, which offered seven grades of salt that ranged from "kurkutch" (extra coarse) to "extra fina" (extra fine). The report touted the Torrevieja salt's worldwide reputation for excellence, noting that solar precipitation (a process of drying the salt in the sun) ensured "regular equality of grain, whiteness, and very high saline content."

sageway between the two wharves. The 1884 pact is still in effect today.

As the century came to a close, the Proprietors faced the daunting challenge of surviving in an industry that was declining in importance. The once-thriving waterfront, where Union Wharf had made its home for more than one hundred years, was no longer the city's economic anchor. Since rebuilding after the Fire of 1866, Portland had shifted its focus from Commercial Street to Middle Street. There, new electric streetcars carried commuters and shoppers to a burgeoning retail and office district. Roads and rails had replaced the waterfront as the lifeblood of the community.

IV

Port In Decline

T he twentieth century brought dramatic changes that altered forever the way people communicated, traveled, performed their work, and entertained themselves. In 1900 American scientist R.A. Fessenden transmitted human speech over radio waves for the first time. By the end of the decade, the Wright brothers had made their historic flight in Kitty Hawk, North Carolina; the first Model T had rolled off Ford Motor Company's production lines; and the Panama Canal split two continents in half. Telephones, radios, television sets, and cars would be commonplace in almost every American home by mid-century.

The composition of the American people changed, too, as more than ten million people from southern and eastern Europe sought a better life in the United States between 1905 and 1914. Many of these new Americans settled in Portland and worked along the docks to support their families.

Portland's waterfront, which had for more than two centuries relied on ancient modes of transportation and manual labor, found it difficult to keep pace with the rapid changes occurring. A special state commission authorized to study the Portland waterfront in 1907 concluded that the wharves were "many decades behind the times," lacking modern, fireproof facilities.

In 1901, exports far outweighed imports in the port. Shipments of grain, apples, cheese, meats, flour, canned goods, cattle, and sheep—to the tune of $45.5 million—left Portland Harbor that year. Only a meager $9.3 million worth of imports—mostly salt, coal, iron, sugar, and china clay and bleaching powder used in the paper industry—came into the port. Without the lucrative molasses imports filling their hulls on the return trip to Portland, the port's ships found it difficult to compete with trains and trucks. Canadian trade disappeared when St. John, New Brunswick, developed a rival winter port that robbed Portland of its standing as the region's leading seaport. Because of the imbalance of imports and exports and the rising wages for longshore workers, it cost more to put cargo aboard a vessel at Portland than it cost to ship the cargo between Portland and New York.

As the importance of the port declined, city officials

turned landward to bolster Portland's economy. They began to focus on tourism and manufacturing as sources of income for the city's inhabitants.

Through it all, Union Wharf managed to remain profitable by continuing to attract diverse tenants and by investing in real estate. These investments began in 1902 when the Proprietors bought neighboring Widgery's Wharf and a number of its buildings. Union and Widgery's had been the center of the rum-and-molasses trade in the nineteenth century. At the height of its glory in those days, Widgery's had been homeport to seventy-five coasters—small, speedy sailing vessels—carrying coal, groceries, sardines, and salt. By 1920, its fleet had shrunk to twenty. The Proprietors also amended their corporate charter to allow them to acquire real estate and personal property in Portland of up to $100,000 in value. The following year, they bought sixteen stores and lots on the east side of Union Wharf for $2,000 to $2,500 each, paid for by issuing $37,000 in bonds.

THE SALT TRADE

The salt and coal trade begun in the late 1800s became the wharf's twin anchors. The salt came primarily from Turks Island, the Bahamas; Spain; and Sicily, Italy. Schooners carrying the salt to Union Wharf made good time in clear weather— about three weeks on average. The same journey took up to three or four months, however, when storms prevailed.

By the early 1900s, when most products were transported by railroad, the arrival of the salt ships into port caused quite a stir. In 1911, the local paper reported that the sight of two square riggers unloading salt on Union Wharf "caused consid-

Salt Ship A-Comin'

Until World War II halted salt shipments by sea, salt-bearing vessels regularly sailed to Union Wharf from Turks Island in the Bahamas, Spain, and Sicily, Italy. The arrival of the huge masted ships at Union Wharf, after days or weeks at sea, was big news and caused quite a stir in port.

In 1900, the Italian barkentine *Arturio D'Ali* "created a sensation along the waterfront with her daring," as Captain Felippo Salvo brought the ship in during thick fog without a tugboat leading the way, even though he had never been in the port before. Salvo claimed his intuition warned him when he was near shoals or other dangers. Salvo also distinguished himself by twice completing the trip from Trapani, Sicily, to Portland in forty-eight days, the fastest such journey in thirty years.

J.A. McIver, captain of the salt schooner *James W. Elwell*, earned fame as the keeper of a marine menagerie. On his ship he carried a dog, three cats, a fat black pig, a rooster, and a hen. Several other hens that started the 1913 trip from Turks Island never made it to port; they made good eating for the meat-deprived crew.

Some crews used the loading and unloading of heavy salt cargo to prove their stamina. In March 1915, the crew of the schooner *Mary E. Smith* loaded 560 bags of salt in record time. It took the hardy workers just two hours and ten minutes to lift and heave the unwieldy cargo into the ship.

Before vessels could discharge their cargo, they had to

show a bill of health to customs inspectors who greeted them upon their arrival in port. Ships without bills were quarantined before unloading. Port officials feared ships arriving from the West Indies might carry tropical sick-nesses. The public health department fumigated the *James W. Elwell* in 1913 because of the illness of one crewman who was sent to the hospital. A year earlier the three-masted *Silverleaf* arrived from Bonaire and had to be fumigated because of widespread sickness in the West Indies.

Weather played havoc with many vessels traveling between Union Wharf and foreign ports. In 1911 the *Emma Angell*, the second-largest three-masted schooner in the world, was anchored off Ram Island en route to Union Wharf when a gale-force wind cut the main boom in half and split several sails.

The steamship *Annetta*, carrying 847 tons of salt in 1917, survived four days of gales and hurricane-strength winds on a trip from Turks Island to Portland. The storm tore the steering gear apart, flung off doors like paper, and flooded the deck and the quarters of the cook and officers. The damage didn't daunt First Officer Swanson, who had left the crew of the liner *Halifax* two weeks earlier. Shortly after Swanson's transfer, the *Halifax* was torpedoed and sank, claiming all aboard.

Another steamer, the *Anna*, helped rescue the crew of the *Yma*, which was shipwrecked on a West Indies reef during a tropical hurricane in 1919. The *Anna* picked up survivors and brought them to Grand Turks in the Bahamas.

erable commotion among some of the old waterfronters yesterday, as it carried them back to the times when all the commerce at this port was carried on by square riggers."

The W.H. Shurtleff Company stored salt in a large storehouse at the end of Union Wharf. Shurtleff sold most of the salt to the fishing industry, but its diverse customers also included the ice cream industry and the railroads, which used the mineral to keep switches from freezing during the winter.

Until the late 1940s, workers used hand trucks (large dollies) to unload the salt and bagged it by hand. One worker held a bag on a scale while another shoveled in the salt until each bag weighed 100 to 140 pounds. Workers then pulled tie wires tight around the tops of the bags to close them and loaded them onto hand carts, four or five per load. The salt was trundled to the corner of the warehouse, where workers stacked the bags against the wall. Before machinery made the process easier, it took a dozen men to unload the salt from a ship at port.

Salt shipments to Union Wharf waxed and waned with the political climate. Several years before the outbreak of World War I in 1914, shipments became sporadic and salt became a scarce commodity throughout New England. In May 1912 the local paper reported that "an absolute [salt] famine" would exist in Portland save for the arrival at Union Wharf of the bark *Santa Maria* with 1,200 tons from Trapani, Sicily. Several small schooners divided up the precious cargo, vital to the fishing industry, and carried it to Rockland, Vinalhaven, and Gloucester, Massachusetts. Within a month, the largest salt shipment ever from Turks Island—1,800 tons—arrived at Union Wharf.

Italy's entrance into World War I in 1915 shut off all business from Trapani, one of the principal salt ports. Shipments continued from Turks Island but became less regular. In 1916, Union Wharf did not receive its first Turks Island shipment of the year until August. In 1919, the *Huntley Torrevieja* sailed from Turks Island with a large shipment just in time to replenish the nearly empty salt sheds on Union Wharf.

The second decade of the twentieth century marked the beginning of the end for the majestic sailing ships that had for centuries graced Portland's waterfront. For the first time, salt began to arrive by steamer. Importers who did not have enough salt for a full load banded together and chartered a steamship to consolidate their loads. When the Norwegian *Imperator* arrived at Union Wharf on December 11, 1916, it was the fourth cargo of salt brought by steamer in five years. It unloaded at the end of the dock instead of the side because the captain feared he would run aground if he sailed into the shallower slip.

With the shutdown of Italian trade, salt became a commodity in great demand. Prices soared as vessel owners demanded exorbitant fees to bring precious salt to a desperate market. During the war, merchants collected an average of twenty-five cents a bushel to transport salt, a huge jump from the seven-cent fee they had earned. The world war made its mark on the waterfront in other ways as well. Millions of head of cattle and tons of food made its way from Canadian and American farmland to Portland Harbor, where the cargo was shipped to the Allies in Europe. The amount of cargo passing through the port reached its peak at more than three million tons in 1916.

At war's end, salt supplies increased, prices retreated, and

Union Wharf, winter 1975

Parker Poole Jr.'s tugboat, Victoria, in 1977

Old buildings on the wharf were razed in the 1980s to make way for a modern warehouse and a parking lot. Tied up to the wharf at the right is Parker Poole Jr.'s tugboat.

Union Wharf Chandlery & Market, 1992

Parker Poole Jr. stands on the deck outside his Union Wharf office overlooking Portland Harbor in 1997. The Maine Responder, in the center background, is docked at the wharf.

Malcolm Poole, left, and William Poole in 1997

Parker Poole Jr., left, and his son, Charlie Poole, pose in the hallway of the world headquarters of the Proprietors of Union Wharf in 1997. Behind them is a poster commemorating the two hundredth anniversary of the founding of the wharf.

Larry Roe of the Marine Spill Response Corporation, left, and Charlie Poole walk along Union Wharf in 1995. MSRC's 208-foot spill response vessel, the Maine Responder, is pictured to the right.

in 1926 the W.H. Shurtleff Company opened a Bangor port to handle its growing salt business. In 1936, Shurtleff ran a full-page newspaper advertisement announcing the arrival of seven hundred tons of salt direct from Turks Island to Bangor.

The company owned two schooners, the *William Keene* and the *Grace and Alice*, which delivered salt along the Maine coast. The two were among the few remaining sailing vessels still in use at Union Wharf. Launched in 1866, the *William Keene* made the eighty-mile trip from Belfast to Portland in 1939 in the astonishing time of fourteen hours. A steamboat would have been hard-pressed to beat that feat. Local waterfront salts claimed the run, captained by 25-year-old Obed Peabody of Jonesport, was among the speediest ever made by a packet. The usual two-man crew had loaded fifty tons of fertilizer and twenty-five tons of salt aboard the vessel at Union Wharf before heading to Belfast. Captain Peabody was known for making brisk times with the *William Keene*. His father, John, who taught him how to sail, had captained the *Grace and Alice*.

COAL POCKETS

By 1910, many people used coal to heat their homes, cook their meals, and light their streets. Much of the activity that occurred on the forty-six wharves stretched along Commercial Street during this time revolved around coal, lumber, and ice. In 1913, two million tons of coal were shipped to the port.

Coal traveled by steamers and barges to pockets, gigantic holding areas topped by steel towers. In 1914–1915, the Pennsylvania-based Lehigh Coal and Navigation Company built a

An International Mix

Portland was settled mainly by English and Irish immigrants, but like other seaport towns its history included people from various parts of the world. Spanish sailors, so often depicted in the poems of Henry Wadsworth Longfellow, strode the streets. Before the Civil War, blacks commonly worked as stevedores on the piers. Some, like Elbridge Talbot who had a one-quarter share in a ship named *Sara*, became shipmasters. In the late nineteenth century, many Italians came to work on the railroads and stayed to fill other jobs around the docks. In 1914, Italians led a strike at the Grand Trunk Railroad coal pockets on the eastern end of the waterfront. According to the daily paper, some employees wanted to stay on the job but the strikers "stationed at all the approaches to the pockets with clubs in their hands caused a change of heart and all quit work."

pocket at Union Wharf that came to be considered the best in New England. Lehigh, the oldest mining concern in the country, built the pocket on the west side of the wharf over a five-month period. On its first day of operation on Thursday, February 11, 1915, hundreds of people crowded the dock to watch the giant four-hundred-foot crane in action as it hoisted coal into the storage area. Business proved brisk that first day. Coal by the carload left the wharf by rail, while local truckers toted the fuel to homes and businesses around the city.

Both coal and anthracite came from the Pennsylvania region, by way of New York City, on one of Lehigh's thirty-five barges. The pockets could handle up to four thousand tons of coal at a time. They featured the most up-to-date machinery to unload the coal and process it. Numerous bins sorted and screened the cargo, while railroad cars waited below to catch the cleaned coal. Shurtleff shipped the product out by rail around the region, mainly within a hundred-mile radius. The steel structures of the coal pockets dominated Union Wharf's skyline until 1947.

Oil shipments, which began arriving in Portland on a regular basis in the second decade of the century, soon rivaled coal as a major import. By 1933, as much fuel oil was being delivered to the port as coal.

The Great Depression of 1929 hit Portland hard, and for the next dozen years the city and its waterfront businesses concentrated on just staying afloat. A fire on Union Wharf in February 1932 didn't help matters. The three-alarm blaze destroyed the second floor and attic of a large building occupied by W.H. Shurtleff Company at the head of the wharf. The fire, of unknown origin, caused two-thirds of the roof to collapse. As in the fire of 1805, low tide prevented the fire boat from reaching the site. Six hose lines from a boat on the west side and fifteen hoses from land poured water on the flames. The losses totaled $35,000 and included damaged meat scraps, charcoal, and poultry equipment. Offices belonging to Shurtleff and to the Hulse Roofing Company were also destroyed in the fire.

Two days before the fire, William Shurtleff's brother, George, who had served as treasurer of the company for many years, died. William, who had been in failing heath, died two years later. During this time, William's son-in-law, Parker Poole Sr., helped manage the wharf. Sylvan Shurtleff, William's only son, took over the reins of the Shurtleff Company when his father died. Parker Poole Sr. continued to manage Union Wharf and served as president of the wharf corporation. Shortly afterward, Poole became president of W.H. Shurtleff Company as well.

Poole skillfully guided both firms through the hardest of times: the remainder of the Great Depression, the war years that followed, and into the 1950s and 1960s as the port declined. In 1937, the Proprietors tore down one of the last remnants of the maritime shipping days, the eighty-year-old wooden molasses shed on Widgery's Wharf. Hartley Simmons, Widgery's wharfinger for thirty-two years, described the razing as "quite a blow. I passed through that old shed a hundred times a day, checking cargo and attending to all the details of the shipments." The shed, which the press called a "symbol and monument" of the harbor's once-flourishing West Indies trade, held its last molasses shipment in 1929. Thirteen years later, the Proprietors of Union Wharf sold Widgery's Wharf for $26,000.

World War II

The outbreak of World War II in Europe in 1939 caused a flurry of consternation among Portland's marine families. W.H. Shurtleff Company had ordered a cargo of salt, and the vessel had set sail from Europe, headed for Union Wharf just as hostilities began. People waited anxiously at the wharf, fearing the Germans would torpedo the boat, but the ship and

The Poole Family

For the better part of a century, the Poole name has been linked with Union Wharf. The first Poole to be associated with the wharf was Parker Poole Sr., who married William Shurtleff's daughter, Marjorie, in 1920. Parker Poole's family had owned a silk manufacturing operation in the first decades of the twentieth century—the Haskell Silk Mill in Westbrook, Maine—and Parker had called on New York City's finest stores selling the firm's products. The company flourished until Dupont introduced rayon in the 1920s as a cheap substitute for silk. That event and the effects of the Depression sank the Pooles' firm. Soon after, Parker Sr. joined his wife's father's company and quickly climbed the corporate ladder. He managed the wharf during William Shurtleff's last illness, and shortly after Shurtleff's death in 1934, Parker Poole Sr. became president of the Shurtleff Company as well.

With a talent for management and an understanding of global economics, Parker Poole Sr. expanded the business and began consolidating the stock and land owned by the Proprietors of Union Wharf. In 1950, he diversified the Shurtleff Company by entering the field of specialized chemicals. By the 1960s, the Poole family controlled all the stock in the Proprietors of Union Wharf, and the corporation owned all the buildings and lots on the wharf.

During the summers and school vacations in the 1930s and 1940s, Parker's sons, Parker Jr. and William, worked at

Union Wharf; Parker worked on the wharf, and William helped load and unload trucks and bag salt for Shurtleff. As a young boy, Parker Poole Jr. dreamed of shipping out on Shurtleff's last coasting schooner, the *William Keene*, but the firm sold the vessel before Parker was old enough to join the crew.

Instead, Parker Jr. went to war, serving for more than two years with the U.S. Marine Corps' Second Marine Division in the Pacific Theater. In the closing days of World War II, Parker Jr. was among the marines who occupied Nagasaki after the United States dropped the atomic bomb on Japan. "If it weren't for the bomb," Parker says, "I probably wouldn't be here." Returning home, he attended Middlebury College in Vermont, married Victoria Simes, and went to work at W.H. Shurtleff Company.

Also a World War II veteran, William served as a combat engineer with General George Patton's Third Army in Europe. After the war, he received his degree from Dartmouth. Like his brother, William worked in the Shurtleff sales department. Gradually the two young men moved to higher positions. When Parker Sr. died in 1965, William became president of W.H. Shurtleff Company. Parker served as vice president of the firm and was named president of the Proprietors of Union Wharf in 1964. He also began serving as wharfinger of Union Wharf, a title he still relishes today.

Parker Poole Jr. brought his growing family to the wharf on Sundays, where the children amused themselves by running to the top of the salt piles stored in the Shurtleff warehouse and sliding down to the floor below. Son Charlie Poole worked summers as a sternman in a lobster boat off Union Wharf. After graduating from Trinity College in 1977, Charlie worked as associate director of admissions and rowing coach at a Connecticut boarding school. Parker Jr.'s enthusiasm for the new projects planned for the wharf persuaded Charlie to return to Portland in 1983 to become general manager and vice president of Union Wharf. Charlie's brother, Malcolm, graduated from Trinity College and in 1977 joined his uncle at the Shurtleff Company. When the company merged with Monson Industries in 1996, he became vice president and general manager.

As wharfinger, Parker Jr. oversees all phases of operation at Union Wharf. Charlie handles the day-to-day activities on the wharf, making sure tenants are satisfied and maintenance is done as needed. He also runs Brown Ship Chandlery Inc. and its subsidiary, Custom Float Services Inc.

With fifteen grandchildren, Parker Poole Jr. is confident the wharf and its parent corporation, the Proprietors of Union Wharf, will remain in the family.

"They will find opportunities here, as we have," says Charlie Poole of the next generation. "They'll make a living, raise a family. And they, too, will become the stewards of time."

crew made it safely to Portland. Shurtleff ordered no more cargoes of salt until after the war had ended.

With the bombing of Pearl Harbor on December 7, 1941, Portland geared up for the war effort. The waterfront became the center of frenetic activity as workers produced Liberty ships at shipyards across the bay in South Portland. Among them was the SS *John A. Poor*, honoring Portland's trade ambassador of the 1850s. Launched on June 23, 1943, the vessel was torpedoed a month later as it traveled from Boston to Halifax. By the end of the war, thirty thousand Maine workers had made thirty ocean-class vessels for the British and 244 Liberty ships for the American fleet.

World War II gave the city an entirely new personality. Almost overnight, Portland Harbor became the base of operations for the North Atlantic fleet. Merchants did a booming business as sailors on leave and shipyard workers, many of them women who answered the call for wartime laborers, filled the streets and the shops. Navy destroyers and support vessels crowded the port's anchorages.

Throughout the war, the Coast Guard patrolled the harbor daily, looking for signs of U-boats and German sabotage. The Union Wharf Proprietors, fearful that the enemy might ignite the wooden dock and buildings, installed a fence that surrounded the structure. Security personnel demanded an ID badge from anyone wishing to enter the wharf. Everything came to a standstill during emergency blackouts.

The economic boom of the war years evaporated once the war ended. Portland's waterfront continued to decline in importance. As in the earlier war, battles in Europe during World War II had disrupted salt shipments. From then on, salt came by rail only. However, a pipeline built during the war to transport South American crude oil from Portland to Montreal sparked an increase in tanker traffic in the harbor. In 1946 tankers brought 5.9 million tons of oil into the city's port.

END OF AN ERA

Fire finished off another mainstay of Union Wharf, the coal pockets where tons of product had been sorted and stored for reshipment. On December 26, 1947, a five-alarm fire swept through the gigantic coal pockets. The blaze began when gale-force winds blew high-tension wires against the pockets and caused a short circuit. Many observers considered the pockets, owned by Randall & McAllister, the best of their kind in New England.

Raging out of control, the flames brought fire trucks from all over the city to the site. Three thousand tons of coke and anthracite fed the fire. Two Coast Guard cutters tried to reach fishing boats tied up alongside the dock, but the scorching heat kept them back. At 1:16 a.m. the pocket's twelve-foot, four-hundred-ton crane tower, its underpinnings consumed by fire, collapsed and crashed through the hull of one of the boats, the wooden trawler *Jeanne D'Arc*. The eighty-two-foot trawler sank to the bottom of the shallow slip, completely destroyed. The *Jeanne D'Arc* belonged to F.J. O'Hara & Sons, owners of a fish handling plant at the end of Union Wharf.

A thirty-mile-an-hour wind threatened to spread the fire to nearby wharves and other businesses on Union Wharf, but a steady stream of water from fire hoses spared the adjacent buildings.

The midnight blaze headlined the front page of the Portland newspaper the next day. The fire lasted seventeen hours and cost the city $325,000 to fight. In addition to losing the *Jeanne D'Arc*, valued at $55,000, F.J. O'Hara suffered damages of $25,000 to three other fishing trawlers. Randall & McAllister lost $300,000 in the fire. The flames completely destroyed the pockets and marked the end of Union Wharf's coal storage and shipment business.

The further decline of the sea trade forced Union Wharf and Commercial Street property owners to seek out a diverse mixture of land-based tenants. The brick row buildings near Union Wharf housed grocery wholesalers such as Milliken, meat packers such as Swift and Cudahy, and coal dealers such as A.R. Wright Company and Pocahontas Fuel. These businesses all made use of the railroads that ran outside their doors and down along the wharves.

At Union Wharf, Maine Marine Products, a poultry supply company, built a plant in 1950 on the space formerly occupied by the coal pockets. Maine Marine produced fish meal, which was used to feed chickens. Live chickens kept by the company as taste testers were among the more raucous occupants of Union Wharf. They spent their time clucking, tasting meal, and laying eggs.

Other tenants in the mix included Hulse Roofing Company; sailmakers Leavitt & Parris, on the wharf from 1919–1981 and still in business today; the W.D. Demmons Corporation, tinworkers; and the Charles Chase Company, a dealer in household materials such as cement and plaster. The A. Herman Bag Company, located on the wharf from 1930–1981, printed seventy to eighty kinds of bags for potato companies

Historic Model

In 1962 the National Park Service measured the W.H. Shurtleff storehouse to provide a model for the historic recreation of a salt shed and warehouse from the late 1700s and early 1800s. The building still contained a wooden hoist, with a rope that ran through a hole between the first and second floors. By pulling on the rope, which was wrapped around the hoist wheel, a laborer on the first floor was able to hoist a load weighing tons up to the second floor.

around New England. During its heyday, the firm produced fifteen thousand bags a day.

Union Wharf continued to house marine businesses as well. F.J. O'Hara & Sons operated its fish packing business at the end of the wharf. The Maine Fish Meal Company rented wharf space, and the firm of John Flaherty built a fish market on Commercial Street at the head of the wharf in the early 1940s. The dominant business on the dock remained the W.H. Shurtleff Company, which occupied the large building fronting Commercial Street at 1 Union Wharf until 1964.

The W.H. Shurtleff Company underwent many transformations during its long career on Union Wharf. When World War II put a halt to deliveries of salt via the ocean, Shurtleff shipped rock salt by railroad car from New York, Ohio, and Louisiana. A new technological age introduced machinery to the wharf that eliminated much of the sweat labor required of earlier salt workers. Crews still had to shovel salt, but they dumped it onto portable conveyors that automatically poured the crystals into bags. Later, shoveling became unnecessary with the use of rail cars that deposited their salty cargo directly onto the conveyor belt. The new system required half the manpower needed in the past.

The loading platforms at Shurtleff's warehouses, dating back to the nineteenth century, had been built ten to twelve inches off the ground to accommodate horse-drawn delivery wagons. Shurtleff had to install false floors or use ramps to load the twentieth-century trucks that delivered salt and other products to the regional market.

In 1950, Shurtleff entered the growing field of industrial chemicals, importing calcium chloride and soda ash by rail. The company handled a cornucopia of other products as well, including milk bottles, oyster shells, and signposts. In 1964, Shurtleff transferred its headquarters to nearby Richardson Wharf, which the Proprietors of Union Wharf had bought the year before. Shurtleff retained a salt storehouse on Union Wharf. The company later moved to South Portland when the city took over Richardson Wharf to build the publicly financed Portland Fish Pier.

In the 1950s, the Shurtleff-Poole family began to buy out the other shareholders. The Shurtleff family had been a major shareholder in the Proprietors of Union Wharf since the 1800s. Of twenty-eight shares, nine were owned by Marjorie Shurtleff Poole, who had inherited them from her father, W.H. Shurtleff. Her husband, Parker Poole Sr., bought out the remaining shareholders, and by 1960 the Proprietors of Union Wharf belonged solely to the Shurtleff-Poole family.

Over the same period, the wharf corporation began buying lots on the wharf owned by individual businesses. In addition to her shares in the corporation, Marjorie Poole had inherited the twelve buildings occupied by the Shurtleff Company on the wharf. Parker Poole Sr. negotiated the purchase of the final lots on the wharf owned by people outside the family. When Poole's son, Parker Poole Jr., took over as president in 1964, the Proprietors of Union Wharf—now his family's firm—owned the entire wharf and rented the space to various businesses, including several owned by the corporation itself. The seven current-day proprietors are all Shurtleff descendants. Parker Poole Jr.; his brother, William Poole; and Parker's sons, Malcolm Poole and Charlie Poole, are all involved in the operations of the Proprietors of Union Wharf. Parker's other children, Alexandra Sawyer, Christina Thomas, and Parker Poole III, own stock but are not actively involved in the corporation.

TEARING DOWN, BUILDING UP

In 1961, the *Portland Press Herald* ran a series called "Our Crumbling Waterfront," detailing the deterioration of the port. The series gave a stark description of rotting pilings, empty buildings, and shattered dreams along the bay.

The Proprietors of Union Wharf were determined to prevent their property from sharing the fate of neighboring docks long since abandoned. Parker Poole Jr. orchestrated efforts to tear down deteriorating buildings on the wharf and renovate the ones remaining. Poole began by demolishing the wharf's older, fire-prone buildings that had outlived their purposes.

This included the last eighteenth-century structure on the waterfront: four abutting warehouses that had once been used to store salt and coal. The complex was bulldozed in 1969. Removal of the decaying older buildings on the wharf continued into the 1990s.

The wharf itself also received needed attention. In the early 1970s the Proprietors filled in part of the slip area to reclaim eight thousand square feet of usable land. New pilings provided a secure base for the wharf.

With its rehabilitation well under way, Union Wharf remained a busy place. In 1971 thirty stores occupied the wharf, and almost every building not under construction was full. When a major tenant, Maine Marine Products, chose not to renew its $14,000 per year lease in 1968, Marine Repair Inc. filled the void. The repair shop leased a twenty-one-by-seventy-foot lot plus dock space in 1969. A Coca Cola Bottling plant rented several lots and a truck platform that had formerly been occupied by the Charles Chase Company.

As it had done for almost two centuries, Union Wharf remained profitable by responding to changing conditions, making improvements, and attracting new tenants. But by the early 1970s, as other wharves decayed around them, the Pooles wondered how long Portland's waterfront could survive. Without a turnaround, they knew business owners would be reluctant to locate in this deteriorating section of town. As Parker Poole Jr. noted in a magazine article on Portland's waterfront, "People don't invest unless there's a return."

V

Renovation and Renewal

For the next decade things got a lot worse along the waterfront before they got better. More than one person noted that the waterfront was on "the wrong side of the tracks" in the 1960s and 1970s.

The only bright spot occurred at the west end of the waterfront, the site of the International Marine Terminal. With help from the state and federal government, the city built the terminal in 1970 at the request of Lion Ferry Company Ltd., a Swedish firm that planned to run a ferry between Portland and

Yarmouth, Nova Scotia. Located on the site of the old Portland Terminal Company's cargo pier, the marine terminal represented the largest expenditure of public funds for a waterfront project since the construction of the Maine State Pier in 1923.

While the development of the marine terminal offered a ray of hope for waterfront businesses, the overall picture of the harbor was one of overwhelming gloom. A 1977 report in the Portland newspapers found little change from the port's "crumbling" image of the 1960s. According to the study, 37 percent of all waterfront buildings were rundown and eleven of twenty piers were below standard. There was little parking for the three thousand or so waterfront workers along congested Commercial Street, where railroad cars and trucks vied with automobiles for travel lanes.

Between 1978 and 1983, Portland Harbor was the subject of twenty-five studies, as city officials pondered the changing nature of Commercial Street and what to do with its aging wharves. A 1978 study funded by the National Science Foundation described Portland's waterfront as one of the most decrepit on the East Coast.

The condition of the bay was even worse. Sixteen million gallons of raw sewage and industrial waste spewed into the harbor every day from unregulated sewer pipes. Cleanup crews retrieved eighty tons of debris from Casco Bay in a year.

Jack MacDiarmid, who toured Portland in 1969 as a representative of Republic Steel, told a local business magazine he remembers thinking, "How could anybody live here?" MacDiarmid later became president of the Chamber of Commerce of the Greater Portland Region.

OLD PORT RENAISSANCE

The resurrection of Portland's waterfront can be traced to two occurrences: the redevelopment of the Old Port area of the city in the late 1970s and 1980s and the passage by the U.S. Congress of the Magnuson Act in 1976.

Beginning in the mid 1970s, forward-thinking developers began restoring the rundown historic buildings in the city's Old Port area between Congress Street and the central waterfront. The area soon became the center of booming economic activity, with small shops vying for space with restaurants, bars, law firms, and other professional offices. By the 1980s, the Old Port had blossomed into a mecca for tourists, and the search for space had spread to Commercial Street.

Encouraged by the economic activity around them, the Proprietors of Union Wharf began renovation projects of their own. Beginning in 1983 the Proprietors created a 125-car parking lot by demolishing the buildings on twelve lots on the east side of the wharf. Portland Economic Development Director Clark Neily said the city was "very grateful" for the new lot, which provided needed parking space in the area. The destruction of the nineteenth-century buildings, however, forced several old-time tenants to relocate. The Leavitt & Parris awning and canvas company had been on Union Wharf since 1919, and the A. Herman bag business since 1930. Another displaced tenant, Popeye's Takeout, had provided snacks there since 1975.

During the same period, city officials convinced Bath Iron Works to locate its new shipbuilding complex and drydock along the eastern part of the waterfront at the Maine State Pier,

Parker Poole's 'Marvelous Project'

For ten years, the tugboat *Victoria* became a fixture of Union Wharf. The seventy-foot tug was built in Mahone Bay, Nova Scotia, in 1945 as part of a fleet destined for the European Theater during World War II. The war ended before the boat was shipped, and the tug took on peacetime duties on the St. Lawrence River.

Parker Poole Jr. spotted the well-worn tug in the classified ad section of a boating magazine in 1973. A ride in Mahone Bay was all it took for him to fall in love with the vessel, even in its deteriorated state. "It was a wreck," Poole recalled. The only condition he placed on the sale was that the seller deliver the tug to Union Wharf, a feat easier said than done.

The crew got lost and had no electricity on board, but the tug made it to Portland under its own power. The boat,

which had closed in 1981. During marathon negotiations, the city agreed to buy the fifty-eight-acre site from the state, build a new six-hundred-foot pier to the east of the current structure, and lease it to BIW for the next twenty years. The city and state each provided $15 million toward the cost of the project, with BIW supplying the remaining $20 million. It was the most expensive project ever financed by the state's taxpayers. Lured by the promise of one thousand new jobs, city and state officials signed the agreement with BIW on August 1, 1981.

The west end of the waterfront had its own excitement.

which Parker renamed for his wife, Victoria, cost him $5,000 plus $100 in duty fees.

"I always wanted a tugboat," Poole said. He spent the next four years renovating the vessel. Poole's "marvelous project" required a rebuilt pilot house and a new engine. Workers had to use eight thousand pounds of rock for ballast when they replaced the old fifteen-ton Lathrop engine with a GM model.

For six years Poole toured the Maine coast in the rejuvenated tug. In 1983, he donated it to a youth organization. Photos of the tug remain on Poole's Union Wharf office wall, including a sequence of the vessel's misadventure in Stonington, Maine, where it hit a rock just as the tide was receding. Poole had to wait through an entire cycle until the tide reached its peak and the tug bobbed up and off the rock. Shuddering at the memory, Poole said, "That was a dark day."

Paul E. Merrill, who had begun his business with a secondhand Reo truck and developed it into a multimillion-dollar trucking firm, turned his attention to the waterfront. In 1977, he drew up plans for a $12 million cargo pier. Before his death in 1982, he watched as the pier's first delivery—a load of coal—arrived at Merrill's Marine Terminal. It was Portland's first large shipment of coal since the 1940s.

A multimillion-dollar sewer project, financed largely with federal money, helped clean up Casco Bay. Once reeking with pollution, the harbor became a sparkling tourist destination.

TWO-HUNDRED-MILE FISHING LIMIT

The second event that stimulated development along Portland's waterfront was the passage of the Magnuson Fisheries Conservation and Management Act, also known as the Two-Hundred-Mile Limit Law. The regulation banned fishing by foreigners within two hundred miles of the U.S. coast. Passed as a way to protect fisheries stock from overharvesting by the huge, factory vessels operated by the Soviets and other foreigners, the law enticed thousands of U.S. citizens into the fishing business.

The long-neglected waterfront now attracted intense interest from two sources: developers who wanted to convert piers and docks into condominiums, hotels, and shops; and a growing number of fishermen who wanted to ensure access to the water and who needed more berthing space for their boats.

In 1977, a group of fishermen stormed City Hall. They demanded the city's help in upgrading the waterfront for marine-based businesses and providing berthing space for their boats. Without such help, they warned, Portland's fishing industry would disappear. City officials were sympathetic. So were the state's voters. In 1979, they approved a $9 million bond to help pay for a fish pier in Portland and smaller piers in several other communities.

With additional help from a federal economic development grant, the city built the Portland Fish Pier, a $17 million complex that provided berthing and offloading for commercial fishing boats. The fish pier also featured the Portland Fish Exchange, a fish distribution center with the only display fish auction in the continental United States. Completed in 1983, the city-owned complex occupies almost twenty acres of prime waterfront property.

During initial discussions about the fish pier, city officials proposed building it at the site of Union Wharf. "I just went wild," Parker Poole Jr. said later, recalling his fury over what he considered a preposterous proposal. In the end, the city took a number of smaller wharfs, including Richardson Wharf, by eminent domain for the project. Richardson Wharf, owned by the Proprietors of Union Wharf, was the home of the W.H. Shurtleff Company. In June 1982 Shurtleff relocated to South Portland, where the firm operates from an office/warehouse complex on ten acres of land on Runway Road. Parker Poole Jr.'s brother, William, and Parker's son, Malcolm, run Shurtleff, which merged with the Proprietors of Union Wharf in 1983 and became a wholly owned subsidiary of the corporation. The firm handles such products as rock salt, calcium chloride pellets, culverts, plastic pipe, and sanitary water controls.

All along the waterfront, new construction projects replaced the rotting pilings and crumbling piers of the previous decade. Spurred by the development of the Portland Fish Pier, private fishermen joined together to purchase Hobson's Wharf and renovate it. Berlin Mills Wharf, to the west of the fish pier, became the home of Gowen Inc.'s boat repair business. Accountant Samuel Davidson and fisherman Robert Tetrault began plans for construction of a $1.7 million office complex on the Portland Fish Pier known as the Marine Trade Center. Other fishermen united to form Vessel Services Inc., an oil and ice supplier that also located on the fish pier.

Union Wharf undertook its own major construction project during the early 1980s. The Proprietors installed a twelve-inch, gravity-fed sewer line along the length of the wharf. The project provided a look into the past as contractors peeled back the centuries-old layers covering the wharf. Beneath the wharf's paved surface lay a corduroy road, a row of huge logs that had been placed there in the 1700s. The logs had provided support for wagons carrying rocks and other materials used as fill for the wharf. Modern building tools proved to be no match for the massive logs. Workers attacked the road with chain saws, but they had to replace the blades several times before the way was finally cleared for the sewer pipe. Where the original builders had used horses and wagons to bring in fill and tamp it down, the modern-day crew shot a laser beam along the wharf to ensure that the sewer pipe lay straight. As Parker Poole Jr. often notes, times do change.

A BRIGHT FUTURE

In their 1982 annual report, the Proprietors predicted a bright future for the waterfront with the construction of the Portland Fish Pier and BIW's new operation. Union Wharf, they noted, was in an "ideal area for future development." Parker Poole Jr. proposed building a chandlery at 1 Union Wharf in 1983 as "just a beginning. We've been doing a lot of tearing down. Now we want something to rejuvenate a bit," he told the *Evening Express.*

Chandleries originally made and sold candles to ships. Later, the marine shops diversified into foodstuffs, ropes, and other necessities for a ship voyage. To house the chandlery, the Proprietors put up a new, two-and-one-half-story brick building at the head of the wharf fronting Commercial Street. The architectural style of the $250,000 structure resembled the historic brick, turn-of-the-century buildings along Commercial Street. Opened in the spring of 1984, the Union Wharf Chandlery & Market served all types of vessels entering Portland Harbor, including commercial fleets, local fishing boats, and pleasure craft. Crews could choose from a list of provisions that included TV dinners, beer, fruit cocktail, bouillon cubes, cashews, and sundries such as gauze, insecticide, toothpaste, and detergent. The Pooles later discovered, however, that running a grocery business was not their forte. In 1991 they turned the company over to Stillwater Corporation, which runs the market today and pays rent for its wharf space.

WATERFRONT ZONING RESTRICTIONS

With so much attention focused on the waterfront, city officials began to realize they needed to develop an overall strategy for renovating the port and controlling growth there. They hired the American City Corporation, whose parent company had designed Boston's Faneuil Hall Marketplace and Baltimore's Harbor Place, to come up with a plan for Portland's deteriorating waterfront. The ACC plan, made public in December 1981, called for construction of a $2.8 million ferry terminal at the end of Custom House Wharf to serve Casco Bay islanders, several parking garages, two office complexes, and townhouse condominiums on Long Wharf and Central Wharf. The $65 million redevelopment package also recommended building a 275-room hotel, a parking garage, and a fishermen's memorial park along Commercial Street at the head of Widgery's and Union wharves.

For all its ambitious ideas, the ACC plan made no provision for new berthing space or for protection of marine businesses. Visions of condominiums, hotels, and a convention center on the waterfront fueled fear that fishermen and marine businesses would be squeezed out as land fetched higher prices for other uses. The plan met with immediate protests from proponents of a working waterfront. Wharf owners, business people, fishermen, and others quickly formed the Waterfront Preservation Association to oppose implementation of the plan.

City officials responded to the criticism by eliminating some features of the ACC plan and crafting a new zoning code that divided the waterfront into two zones: W-1, which allowed a variety of uses, and W-2, which was reserved for marine uses. The City Council adopted the code in early 1983. The W-1 zones, where condominiums, hotels, and shops as well as marine businesses were allowed, included the four wharves opposite the Old Port area—Central (now Chandler's), Long Wharf, Portland Pier, and Custom House Wharf. Areas in the W-2 zone, which included Union Wharf, could be occupied only by marine-related businesses.

The Pooles had mixed feelings about the city's new zoning ordinance. Parker Poole Jr. heartily agreed that it was important to keep the port for commercial marine uses. "Portland Harbor should be commercial," he said in an interview in a local business magazine. "It's the best deepwater harbor on the eastern seaboard." But Charlie Poole noted that marine businesses also needed flexibility in order to maintain their property. One of Portland's strengths, he said, was the diversity of its business community. "It's nice to have a mix. Then you don't have all your eggs in one basket."

Unfortunately, the new zoning ordinance did not provide flexibility for businesses in the marine-only zones. In 1984, Union Wharf found itself among the first waterfront property owners to be targeted for not complying with the ordinance. Filing suit against the Proprietors of Union Wharf in Superior Court, the city contended that two wharf tenants, Dearborn & Whited engineering firm and real estate firm Town & Shore Associates, were not marine-related. The Proprietors argued that the ordinance as written required only that a majority of a wharf's tenants be marine-related; at the time, 95 percent of Union Wharf's tenants were marine businesses.

Parker Poole Jr. told reporters covering the case that the ordinance made it difficult to earn a reasonable rate of return on waterfront property. With interest rates at nearly 17 percent and utility and maintenance costs skyrocketing, waterfront property owners needed all the tenants they could get in order to cover expenses and pay taxes. Limiting potential tenants to one type of business seriously undercut wharf owners' ability to fill vacant offices and rent empty space. Throughout Union Wharf's history, Poole noted, almost all the tenants had been tied to the water. In 1983 the wharf's tenants included a fish company, a fish market, four lobster companies, a marine engine repair business, two marine supply companies, a marine welding company, and twenty to thirty lobster and fishing boats. The city, though not agreeing with the Proprietors, eventually dropped the suit.

The owners of the Marine Trade Center soon echoed the Pooles' concern over finding enough marine-based tenants to fill space in their upper floors. Without a more flexible zoning ordinance, they warned, the entire marine zone could fail. The

Portland Planning Board, responding to the waterfront property owners' pleas, agreed to revise the ordinance to allow a wider range of businesses in the W-2 zone until 1990. But the Portland City Council turned down the plan, saying it weakened the marine zone.

Soon the eyes of the entire city would be focused on waterfront zoning. In early 1985, Jane Chee sold Central Wharf to the Liberty Group, a move that would have major repercussions for businesses up and down the waterfront. The developers built an eighty-eight-unit condominium complex on the renamed Chandler's Wharf that attracted immediate bids of up to $300,000 per unit.

Soon after, Eastern Point Associates proposed an office/residential/retail complex to be built near the BIW site. The project became a lightning rod for controversy over how the waterfront should be used. Proponents of a working waterfront argued that the project and others like it would escalate the value of waterfront property above the reach of fishermen and other marine businesses that depended on access to the port. The group, led by Karen Sanford of "Keep the Port in Portland," called for a five-year ban on condos and all other nonmarine uses along the waterfront. They collected enough signatures to force a referendum on the issue.

The Pooles and other wharf owners generally opposed waterfront condos, too, but they argued that a total ban on nonmarine businesses would threaten their livelihoods and ultimately undermine the working waterfront. The Union Wharf Proprietors were among 150 fishermen and others with waterfront interests who signed a petition against the moratorium. The Pooles noted that the wharves had always thrived on mixed uses. Voters sided with the ban-condo forces and approved the referendum in a two-to-one landslide in 1987. The new law, which went into effect on May 5, 1987, placed a moratorium on all development along the waterfront that was not marine-related. It also nullified any chances that restrictions would be eased on upper floors of waterfront property.

As always, the resourceful Proprietors of Union Wharf persevered, despite restrictive zoning. Charlie Poole, who joined his father in 1983 as vice president and general manager of the Proprietors of Union Wharf corporation, began searching for ways to diversify the business. In September 1987, Brown Ship Chandlery, which the Proprietors had purchased in 1984, moved into a new two-story, ten-thousand-square-foot, frame building erected at 36 Union Wharf. Brown Ship, originally located on Maine Wharf, opened its doors in 1941 to serve World War II ships. Later clientele included tankers and tugboat traffic. From its new location, Brown Ship worked with Union Wharf Chandlery & Market to serve lobster boats, the fishing fleet, tankers, and the island residents of Casco Bay.

Sales at Brown Ship Chandlery topped the $1 million mark in 1987. The local fishing industry—now booming because of the influx of new boats—brought additional business to Union Wharf's two chandleries. In the dozen years after the Two-Hundred-Mile Limit Law became effective, the number of boats fishing for cod, haddock, and other species almost doubled in the port. By 1988, more than ninety groundfish boats used Portland Harbor, and the value of the catch had increased tenfold, from $3.4 million in 1976 to $35.8 million in 1987.

Oil cargoes had peaked at 27.2 million tons in 1976. Once the oil crisis hit, however, cargoes dropped precipitously. In recent years, oil imports had begun to increase, reaching ten million tons in 1989. In 1991 construction of a new oil pipeline between Portland and Montreal brought more tankers to the harbor. Their crews shopped at Union Wharf Chandlery & Market, while the ships bought supplies at Brown Ship. The Union Wharf businesses specialized in prompt service, which kept customers coming back. They also established a good working relationship with the tankers' foreign crews, which hailed from ports around the world. Brown's manager, Brooks Colcord, filled an unusually large order in 1989 when the crew of the 1,072-foot-long carrier USS *John F. Kennedy* called. The shipment included seven thousand ears of corn and eight hundred pounds of bananas.

The new businesses provided an anchor for the wharf during the recession that hit in 1991. That year, the Proprietors of Union Wharf posted a net loss. But better times weren't far away. When the zoning moratorium lapsed in 1992, Portland city officials adopted less restrictive rules that allowed waterfront property owners to lease upper-floor offices to nonmarine businesses. Ground-level space was still limited to businesses that required access to the water.

According to Charlie Poole, the entire back section of one building on Union Wharf had remained vacant for seven years, mostly due to restrictive zoning laws. The day after the new regulations went into effect on February 4, 1993, the wharf firm rented an upper-floor office to an artist. Charlie Poole said he didn't expect a flood of applicants for upper-level offices at the wharf, "but at least now the door is open for possibilities."

In 1993, Brown Ship's profits topped $1 million but dipped by one-quarter in 1995 when the number of ships in port declined. To restore flagging sales, the firm began offering additional products, including phone cards, floats, and salt used to preserve fish. Profits climbed again the next year.

To diversify the corporation's business ventures, Charlie Poole oversaw the opening of a new firm on the wharf, Custom Float Services, in 1988. A subsidiary of Brown Ship, Custom Float operates from the same offices as its parent company and has provided a stable source of income for the corporation. The business provides floats to boat owners and pier operators.

UNION WHARF TODAY

Union Wharf has been almost completely renovated in recent years. The only building remaining from before World War II is a one-story, red frame structure built in the 1920s and currently occupied by Gundry's USA, a fish net and marine hardware store. Many of the wooden buildings were so old, Parker Poole Jr. noted, that they had "run out of gas. It [demolition] was the only way to keep the wharf alive."

A handful of nonmarine businesses rent small, second-floor offices along the wharf, but the vast majority of the activity on the dock is directly related to the sea. "We've made a big effort to keep the wharf marine-related," Poole said. Despite the hardships that the zoning moratorium imposed, he still believes in protecting the working waterfront. "Once you give the waterfront up," he said, "you never get it back— it's gone."

The effort to keep the wharf marine-based was rewarded in ways that Parker and Charlie Poole might never have guessed, thanks in part to the 1989 *Exxon Valdez* oil spill in Prince William Sound, Alaska. Following the disastrous spill, Congress passed the Oil Pollution Act of 1990, requiring oil shippers to develop better methods of containing and recovering spilled oil. To comply with the law, the major oil companies established the Marine Spill Response Corporation. MSRC commands a fleet of sixteen vessels, berthed at ports nationwide and ready to respond to oil spills at a moment's notice.

One of MSRC's vessels, the *Maine Responder*, makes its home at Union Wharf. Charlie Poole played a major role in attracting the ship to the wharf, winning the bidding for the MSRC contract over three other contenders. MSRC's twenty-year lease brings the Proprietors of Union Wharf the stability that comes with a reputable, long-term tenant.

The 208-foot oil spill cleanup ship moved to its new berth at the wharf in January 1995. To accommodate the huge vessel, the Proprietors of Union Wharf dredged 3,500 cubic yards of material from around the wharf to create a nineteen-foot-deep channel. They also rebuilt 225 feet along the western edge of the wharf, driving new pilings and replacing the wooden deck with concrete. MSRC occupies offices and stores equipment in an eleven-thousand-square-foot warehouse that the Proprietors of Union Wharf built for the operation.

The project was not without complications. State environmental officials prohibited the dumping of dredge spoils from the channel into the sea. Demonstrating the ingenuity that has kept Union Wharf afloat for more than two centuries, the Pooles mixed the spoils with cement and used the substance to construct the foundation of the warehouse.

In 1991, a local oil response organization, Clean Casco Bay, established its headquarters on Union Wharf as well. The company works with MSRC to prepare for oil spills and coordinate cleanup efforts in the harbor. Portland Pilots, whose employees guide tankers and other big vessels into port, maintains offices in the same building as Clean Casco Bay. The pilots have operated from Union Wharf since 1984.

Other modern-day tenants include Sapporo's, a Japanese restaurant that operates on Union Wharf land to the east of Union Wharf Chandlery & Market; Periwinkle USA, which processes the mollusk for markets in Japan; and Portland Trap Company, a manufacturer of lobster traps. Several lobster dealers, a lobster bait dealer, a life raft firm, two architects, a lawyer, a business broker, and a real estate company also rent space on Union Wharf.

As he looks out over the harbor from his top-floor office in the Brown Ship building—"the world headquarters of the Proprietors of Union Wharf"—Parker Poole Jr. surveys the wharf that has been the lifeblood of his family for five generations. From these windows he has witnessed the ongoing drama of success and failure repeated many times through the years. "The history of Portland Harbor is here," he says. "Portland was the jewel of the East Coast. It was big time, the last big port before taking off for Europe."

For all his regard for history, Parker Poole Jr. delights in the changes that have expanded opportunities in the harbor. Construction of a new Portland-South Portland bridge has opened the inner port to huge ocean-going vessels; cargo shipments have increased every year since the German shipper Hapag-Lloyd set up shop at the International Marine Terminal in 1991, and Merrill's Marine Terminal has expanded its operation. New cruise ships bring passengers from all over the world to Portland's docks. Oil tankers head for Portland Pipe

Line's terminal across the harbor. Sailing ships—not the clippers and square riggers of the past, but the pleasure boats of a new generation—fill the bay.

Under its mantle of years, Union Wharf itself has become a state-of-the-art operation. Charlie Poole punches a few keys on his office computer and reads a message from a ship halfway around the world. He types his answer and within minutes the reply bounces off a satellite and into the captain's waiting computer.

Union Wharf merchants once stood on this same site almost two centuries ago, peering into the fog to see the flags flying atop Portland Observatory. That was the only advance notice they had that a ship would be coming to port. Families waited months to learn the fate of relatives aboard ocean-crossing ships, and anxious merchants never knew when or whether their cargo would make it to shore.

Parker Poole Jr. marvels at the advances made since the wharf's founding in 1793. "There's a huge contrast between past and present," he says. "To me it's mind-boggling."

Union Wharf has undergone so many changes in its two centuries of existence that a casual observer might forget its connection to the past. But dig deep enough and, like the corduroy road buried beneath its surface, one will find testimony of all the years that have passed over the wooden structure that is Union Wharf. The merchants who walked here, the sailors and hard-working laborers, the horsemen and train crews, the shopkeepers and lobstermen, the families fleeing the Great Fire—all have left behind them, in the words of Portland's poet Henry Wadsworth Longfellow, "footprints on the sands of time."

Index

American City Corp. (ACC),
117–118

Bath Iron Works (BIW), 111–112, 120

Blyth, Samuel, 13, 34–37, 39, *44*

Boxer, 34–38, 39, *44*

Brown Ship Chandlery, 15, 100,
121–123, 125

Brown, J.B., 53, 73–74

Burrows, William, 13, 34–38, 39, *44*

Civil War, 16, 65–70, 79, 95
  effect on Maine shippping, 69–70
  and Union Wharf, 66–68

coal trade, 14–15, 24, *49*, 79–80,
  84–85, 94–96, 102–103, 107, 113

Commercial Street, 13, *44, 45*, 53,
  60–61, 63, 70, 71, 73–74, 77, 81,
  94, 103, 104, 110–111, 116–117
  building of, 13, 60–61, 63

Cram, N.O., *44*, 74–75

Custom Float Services, 100, 123

Dash, 13, 22, 32–33, 38–39, 56

Dow, Neal, 64–65

Embargo Act, 13, 26–27, 29–32, 39

Enterprise, 34–38, 39, *44*

Grand Trunk Railway, 13, 59–61, 95

Great Depression, 96–97, 98

Great Fire of 1866, 15, *44*, 70, 71–74,
  76, 81, 126

Kennebec, 56–57

Ilsley, Daniel, 21, 23

International Marine Terminal,
  109–110, 125

Longfellow, Henry W., 35, 53, 65, 95
  poems of, 38, 53, 69, 126

Magnuson Act, 111, 114, 121

McLellan, Arthur, 20, 23, 25, 28

McLellan, Hugh, 20, 23–24, 25–27,
  29, 31

McLellan, Joseph, 20, 23–24, 25–27,
  29, 31–32

McLellan, Joseph Jr., 26–27, 31

McLellan, Stephen, 27–28, 29

McLellan, Thomas, 28

McLellan, William, 22, 25, 28, 29, 51

McLellan, William Jr., 28, 38, 52

Merrill's Marine Terminal, 113, 125

molasses trade, 13, 14, 21, 41–42,
  52–53, 64, 65, 73–74, 75, 77,
  84–85, 97

pirates, 14, 16, 42–43, 50

Poole, Charlie, 17, *47, 93*, 100, 106,
  121–124, 126

Poole, Malcolm, 17, *47, 92*, 100,
  106, 115

Poole, Marjorie Shurtleff, *47, 48*,
  98, 105–106

Poole, Parker Jr., *iv*, 11, 17, 39, *47,
  49*, 78, *90–93*, 98–100, 106–107,
  112–113, 115–116, 118–119, 123,
  125–126

Poole, Parker Sr., 11, 17, *47, 48, 49*,
  97, 98, 105–106

Poole, William, 17, *47*, 78, *92*,
  98–100, 106, 115

Poor, John Alfred, 59–60, 63, 101

Porter, Samuel, 32–33

Porter, Seward, 32–33, 39, 56–57

Portland *(see also Great Fire)*, *ii*, 11–
  13, 15, 17, 21–23, 28, 41, *46*,
  50–53, 57–60, 63–64, 70, 71–74,
  75, 76, 79, 81, 86, 88, 89, *92*, 94,
  95, 96, 97, 100, 101, 102, 125–126
  in Civil War, 65–70
  decline of port, *82*, 84–85, 97,
  106–107, 109–110
  and Embargo Act, 30–32

founding of, 19–21, 25
renaissance of, 111–117
and War of 1812, 32–39
zoning of, 16, 117–123
Portland Board of Trade, 59, 63
Portland Fish Pier, 105, 114–116
Portland Observatory, 29, 37, 126
privateers, 13, 22, 32–33, 34, 50, 56, 69
Prohibition, 64–65, 75
Proprietors of Union Wharf *(see also Union Wharf)*, *vi–vii, viii,* 12– 17, 22–24, 25, 29, 37, 39, *45, 48,* 54– 57, 60–63, 74–75, 77, 79–81, 85, *93,* 97, 98–100, 101, 105–107, 111, 115–116, 119–122, 124–125
incorporation, 14, 62–63
original members, 22–23, 25, 29, 37
present-day members, 106
railroads, 13–16, *45,* 58–61, 63, 75, 79, 81, 85, 88, 95–96, 102, 103, 104–105, 110
Revolutionary War, 12, 20, 25, 30
Richardson Wharf, 16, 105, 115
salt trade, 14, 15, 17, 24, 40, 55, 77– 78, 79–81, 84, 85–89, 94, 97, 99, 100, 101, 104–105, 107, 115, 123
Shurtleff, A(lva) K., 16–17, *47,* 73, 74, 76–77
Shurtleff, George A., *45,* 77–78, 96
Shurtleff, Sylvan, 17, *47,* 76–77
Shurtleff, Sylvan (W.H.'s son), 97
Shurtleff, W(illiam) H., 17, *45–48,* 77–78, 96–97, 98, 105
Shurtleff, W.H., Company, 15, 17, *40, 45, 46, 48,* 77–78, 81, 88, 94, 96–101, 104–106, 115
Smith, David, 21–22, 29
Smith, St. John, 53, 73
Two-Hundred-Mile Limit Law *(see Magnuson Act)*
Union Wharf *(see also related topics),* *vi–vii, viii, 10,* 11–17, *18,* 22–24,

25, 27, 28–29, 31–33, 34, 36–38, 39, *40,* 42, 43, *44–46, 48–49,* 50– 51, 53–64, 71, 73, 74–75, 76, 78– 81, 85, 86– 87, 88–89, *90–93,* 94– 97, 98–100, 101–107, *108,* 111– 113, 115–116, 118–126
building of, 12, 21–23, 24, 55, 116
businesses on, *vi–vii,* 12, 15–17, 23, 24, 27, 29–33, 39, *44–46, 48–49,* 53–55, 64, 66, 73, 74, 76–77, 78–80, 85, 88, *91,* 94– 96, 100, 102–107, 111, 117, 119, 121–125
and Civil War, 66–68
and Embargo Act, 13, 26–27, 30–32
renovation, 15–16, *91,* 106–107, 111, 115–117, 123–124
and War of 1812, 13, 32–39
wharfingers of, 11, 14–15, 23, 24, 28, 29, 39, 55–56, 62–63, 74– 75, 77, 99–100
and zoning, 16, 118–123
Union Wharf Chandlery & Market, 16, *91,* 116–117, 121, 122, 125
War of 1812, 13, 22, 32–39, 41, 42, *44,* 50
waterfront referendum, 120–121
West Indies trade, 12, 14, 21, 23, 38, 41–43, 50–53, 64, 69–70, 75, 77, 80, 81, 86–87, 94, 97
Widgery's Wharf, *vi–vii,* 16, 53, 64, 80, 85, 97
William Keene, 40, 78, 94, 99
World War I, 16, 88–89
World War II, 16, 86, 97, 99, 101– 102, 104, 112, 121, 123
zoning, 16, 117–123